Spotlight on Young Children

Exploring Play

Holly Bohart, Kathy Charner, and Derry Koralek, editors

National Association for the Education of Young Children
Washington, DC

naeyc®

National Association for the Education of Young Children
1313 L Street NW, Suite 500
Washington, DC 20005-4101
202-232-8777 • 800-424-2460
www.naeyc.org

NAEYC Publishing

Chief Publishing Officer
Derry Koralek

Editor-in-Chief
Kathy Charner

Managing Editor
Mary Jaffe

Senior Editor
Holly Bohart

Senior Graphic Designer
Malini Dominey

Associate Editor
Elizabeth Wegner

Editorial Assistant
Ryan Smith

The following are selections published previously in *Young Children,* and the issues in which they appeared: F.M. Carlson, "Rough Play: One of the Most Challenging Behaviors," July 2011; D.J. Leong and E. Bodrova, "Assessing and Scaffolding Make-Believe Play," January 2012; T. Schwarz and J. Luckenbill, "Let's Get Messy! Exploring Sensory and Art Activities With Infants and Toddlers," September 2012; D. Curtis, K.L. Brown, L. Baird, and A.M. Coughlin, "Planning Environments and Materials That Respond to Young Children's Lively Minds," September 2013.

The following selections were published in the May 2014 issue of *Young Children:* G.T. Anderson, A.R. Spainhower, and A.C. Sharp, "'Where Do the Bears Go?' The Value of Child-Directed Play"; Y. Axelrod, "'Todos Vamos a Jugar, Even the Teachers'—Everyone Playing Together"; T. Kinard, "Flying Over the School: Superhero Play—Friend or Foe?"; M.S. McWilliams, A.B. Vaughns, A. O'Hara, L.S. Novotny, and T.J. Kyle, "Art Play: Stories of Engaging Families, Inspiring Learning, and Exploring Emotions"; J. Trawick-Smith, J. Wolff, M. Koschel, and J. Vallarelli, "Which Toys Promote High-Quality Play? Reflections on the Five-Year Anniversary of the TIMPANI Study"; L.D. Wood, "Viewpoint: Holding on to Play: Reflecting on Experiences as a Playful K–3 Teacher."

Memos, with the exception of those by C. Copple, L. Espinosa, M. Mackrain, R. Pica, and J. Sachs, B. Mardell, and D. Ramsey, were published in the May 2014 issue of *Young Children.*

Permissions

"Brown's Properties of Play" on page 93 and column one of "Practical Suggestions for K–3 Settings Based on Play Personalities" on pages 94–95 are reprinted, by permission, from Stuart Brown & Christopher Vaughan, *Play: How It Shapes the Brain, Opens the Imagination, and Invigorates the Soul* (New York: Penguin, 2009, pp. 17–18 and 65–70, respectively).

Photo Credits

Courtesy of article authors: iii (second and third from top), iv (third from top), 5, 7–10, 14, 17, 19, 20, 22, 75, 77, 79, 82, 83, 99, 101, 102, 105, 109 (top), 110 (top), 111, 113, 115

Copyright © Kathy Charner: iv (second from top), 65; Richard Graessle / © NAEYC: 63; Julia Luckenbill: cover (bottom right), iii (top), 1, 30, 34; Karen Phillips: iii (third from bottom), 26, 31, 69; Theodora Jo Pyle: cover (top right); Shari Schmidt: 27, 73; Ellen B. Senisi: cover (left), iii (second from bottom), iv (top, third from bottom), 37, 39, 41, 56, 68, 71, 87, 89–91, 108, 109 (bottom), 110 (bottom); Elaine I-Ling Shen: iii (bottom), 46, 48, 49, 51; Thinkstock: iv (second from bottom, bottom), 98, 107; Susan Woog Wagner / © NAEYC: 59

Credits

Consultant: Cindy Simpson

Library of Congress Control Number: 2015930862

ISBN: 978-1-938113-14-7

Item 2840

On the opening page of the articles, this logo and the numbers indicate which of the 10 NAEYC Early Childhood Program Standards the articles address. This information guides programs for young children ages birth through kindergarten seeking NAEYC Accreditation or improving program quality.

naeyc® 2,3

Contents

Kathy Hirsh-Pasek and Roberta Michnick Golinkoff

Introduction

Four-year-old Jared and his teacher, Mary, look at the pile of multicolored blocks that are pregnant with possibilities. "Let's build an airport," Jared suggests. Mary becomes Jared's assistant contractor: "You started the second floor of the airport when you put the blue block *on top of* the green block!"

The entire class sits riveted as Mr. Fernandez tells the story of a fire-breathing dragon and its attempt to enter the royal castle. After the story, the children play with toy dragons, castles, and even the proverbial damsel in distress. Vocabulary words like *shield, moat, damsel,* and *crenulations*—introduced and explained by Mr. Fernandez during the story—roll off the tongues, if imperfectly, of the 5-year-olds at play!

Decades of research suggest that children learn best when they are **active** (rather than passive), are **engaged** (not distracted), and find an activity **meaningful,** and when an activity is **socially interactive** (Hirsh-Pasek et al., forthcoming; Chi 2009). Play embodies each of these characteristics. Thus, it should be a top choice among educational pedagogies. Of late, however, play has become a four-letter word. Professor Ed Zigler, often called the father of Head Start, and Sandra Bishop-Josef warn that play is under siege (Zigler & Bishop-Josef 2009). The climate for play and playful learning has become so eroded that one teacher in the article by Trawick-Smith and colleagues (see p. 66 in this volume) notes, "I avoid using the P-word."

This volume is testimony to the value of playful learning and its rightful place among educational approaches in early education. Play and learning are not antithetical, but are integrally connected. The debate about *either* educational classrooms or playful classrooms must be resolved in a way that respects the contributions of both to children's development. It is in block play that Mary, above, introduces those spatial words like *on top of, in, under, next to,* and *beside* that will support later spatial and mathematical ability (Ferrara et al. 2011). It is through play that children try on new words just as they try on the costumes that transform them into knights and dragons and damsels.

The waves of educational history have both celebrated a whole-child, playful approach to learning and argued that playful learning robs children of their academic potential (Bishop-Josef & Zigler 2011; Zigler, Gilliam, & Barnett 2011). In the mid-1950s, with Piaget's and Vygotsky's theories prominent, play was considered the "work of childhood"—the arena in which children learn to solve problems and understand social rules. By 1957, the tide turned as headlines boasted the launch of the Soviet satellite *Sputnik*. Americans had to be prepared to compete in the new world order; academics and science were key, and play was a waste of time.

Benjamin Bloom's classic *Stability and Change in Human Characteristics* (1964) reinforced this academic orientation in early childhood, proclaiming that IQ at 4 years of age accounted for a large portion of the variability in children's later learning. But studies soon showed that IQ was not as malleable as believed, and in the 1970s and '80s the pendulum shifted in favor of developmentally appropriate education. The move toward academic orientation resurfaced with the No Child Left Behind Act of 2001 and with mountains of research on young children showing that differences in learning trajectories are evident well before children stand on the doorstep of formal education.

What is an educator to do with this push and pull, with diametrically opposed philosophical positions? Perhaps it is time to reconcile the differences and to realize that we can have a strong curricular program while endorsing a playful pedagogy. Several prominent scholars have come to the same conclusion. In her "Memo to a Primary Grade Principal" on page 96 in this volume, Marilou Hyson concludes that "play is not a break from learning, but a pathway toward learning." And Lynn Kagan and Amy Lowenstein comment, "The literature is clear: Diverse strategies that combine play and more structured efforts are effective accelerators of children's readiness for school and long-term development" (2004, 72).

We must invest in playful learning that includes both free play and guided play. In both free and guided play, the child directs her own actions and creates her own plot lines. In guided play, however, children do this within adult-supported contexts, such as in Montessori classrooms (Lillard 2013), or with the assistance of an adult who follows their lead and scaffolds the play to a deeper level. The opening vignettes—Jared and Mary co-constructing the play around a block-building project and the play that emerges from the circle time reading in Mr. Fernandez's class—are both examples of guided play. As these teachers introduce and use spatial and language concepts in the context of play and storytelling, the concepts become real and understandable to children.

While there are many benefits to free play (Gray 2013), our own work suggests that when there is a learning goal in mind, guided play trumps free play in achieving learning outcomes. And recent reviews of the literature on free play (Lillard et al. 2013; see also Golinkoff et al. 2013) also suggest that free play, while critically important for young children, might not provide children with the full learning benefits that emerge through guided play. Guided play preserves the child-directedness of play along with the joy of learning while also subtly supporting children as they move toward specified learning goals. It offers a midground position between direct instruction and playful learning, a way to design a strong curricular approach to learning that includes an optimal pedagogical approach for young children.

This book demonstrates how playful learning and guided play can spark a new era in early childhood educational reform. It is time to create learning environments that are active, engaging, meaningful, and socially interactive. In these environments, children will learn math and reading, social studies and science. But they will also learn something that might be even more precious and more important in school and throughout life: how to learn, attend, problem solve, and create. And that is a recipe for success in a fast-paced, global world.

Kathy Hirsh-Pasek, PhD, is the Stanley and Debra Lefkowitz Distinguished Faculty Fellow in the Department of Psychology at Temple University. She has authored 11 books and more than 200 publications.

Roberta Michnick Golinkoff, PhD, University of Delaware, has won numerous awards for her work in developmental science and authored more than 150 articles and 12 books.

In "Let's Get Messy! Learning Through Art and Sensory Play," **Trudi Schwarz** and **Julia Luckenbill** suggest strategies for planning an infant and toddler curriculum that includes art and sensory activities, encouraging experimentation while supervising exploration, and affirming the *process* of such activities for young children.

Deb Curtis, Kasondra L. Brown, Lorrie Baird, and **Anne Marie Coughlin** observe and document toddlers' use of their "remarkable brains" in "Lively Minds at Play: Planning Environments and Materials That Support the Way Young Children Learn." The authors offer principles for choosing materials that encourage toddlers' expansive learning capacities.

Research provides evidence of the positive effects that well-developed, adult-supported play has on children's development. In "Assessing and Scaffolding Make-Believe Play," **Deborah J. Leong** and **Elena Bodrova** provide strategies for assessing the levels of preschool children's independent play to determine the appropriate level of teacher scaffolding.

In "'Where Do the Bears Go?' The Value of Child-Directed Play," **Genan T. Anderson, Anita Rae Spainhower,** and **Ann C. Sharp** illustrate the ways child-directed play stories enable preschoolers to problem solve, make decisions, and self-regulate.

In "Flying Over the School: Superhero Play—Friend or Foe?," **Timothy A. Kinard** analyzes superhero play in preschool and addresses the philosophical, psychological, sociological, and anthropological foundations of such play.

Ysaaca Axelrod's "'Todos Vamos a Jugar, Even the Teachers'—Everyone Playing Together" describes the activities and interactions in a Head Start classroom where teachers support culturally and linguistically diverse children's dramatic play.

The TIMPANI Study—Toys That Inspire Mindful Play and Nurture the Imagination—is a five-year investigation of play materials children use in preschool. In "Which Toys Promote High-Quality Play? Reflections on the Five-Year Anniversary of the TIMPANI Study," **Jeffrey Trawick-Smith, Jennifer Wolff, Marley Koschel,** and **Jamie Vallarelli** discuss their findings and the implications for teachers and families.

A collage-caricature artist inspired "Art Play: Engaging Families, Inspiring Learning, and Exploring Emotions." Authors **M. Susan McWilliams, Ashley Brailsford Vaughns, Anne O'Hara, Loretta S. Novotny,** and **Theodora Jo Kyle** explore strategies for intentionally guiding children's learning through art play in preschool through third grade and introducing vocabulary with activities related to children's books.

In "Holding on to Play: Reflecting on Experiences as a Playful K–3 Teacher," **Lisa D. Wood** shares her views on the importance of play and provides practical ways for early childhood educators to support children's play and communicate its value to others.

Access to play spaces in the United States is impacted by disparities related to race, class, and gender. In "Play for All Children: Access to Quality Play Experiences as a Social Justice Issue," **Olga S. Jarrett, John Sutterby, Darlene DeMarie,** and **Vera Stenhouse** summarize several research studies on play and provide information to raise awareness regarding play experiences in kindergarten and primary classrooms.

"Big Body Play: Understanding and Supporting It" focuses on play that is vigorous, intense, and rough. **Frances M. Carlson** addresses misconceptions about such play and provides strategies for supporting it for children from infancy through third grade.

Memo to: Students in Early Childhood Education Programs

From: Stuart Reifel

Date: January 2015

Subject: The Definition of Play

In your educational and classroom experiences, you are likely to find that definitions of play serve various purposes, depending on the audience. I might define and use the word *play* in different ways depending on whether I am doing research, addressing classroom teachers, leading a graduate student discussion, or lecturing undergraduates—such as you. Undergraduates are learning that play supports young children's learning in content areas. Teachers seek scholarly explanations of play to support their practices. Graduate students and scholars try to craft new knowledge that relates to scholarly definitions of play. Same word; differing meanings.

I have been guided in this by early childhood theorists who include play as part of their agendas—for example, Vygotsky, Bruner, Piaget, Bateson, Sutton-Smith. In thinking about classroom play in particular, Vygotsky's writings on play and, more important, on what he teaches us about how we acquire concepts have been great influences.

Stuart Reifel, EdD, is professor emeritus at The University of Texas at Austin, where he conducted research and taught about play for more than 30 years. Now retired, he continues his writing and lecturing.

Each article in this collection includes a feature titled **Families and Play,** in which authors offer suggestions for ways teachers can partner with and encourage families to value and foster playful learning both at home and in the early childhood setting.

Knowing that there are numerous definitions of play and its role in young children's development and learning, we invited several early childhood educators to write their own definitions. You will find them throughout this book, written in the form of memos to various audiences. We hope these thoughts inspire you to consider how you might define the role of play in the early childhood years.

The book closes with a study guide by Peter Pizzolongo that poses questions to expand on the content of each article. Readers can reflect on the questions alone, talk about them with colleagues, or discuss them as participants in a class or workshop led by a facilitator. The guide begins with "Recalling Your Own Early Experiences," which asks readers to think about their own play experiences. The section "Expanding on Each Article" includes a brief summary of each article and specific questions and follow-up activities. In the last section of the study guide, "Making Connections," readers consider the big picture, examine their curricula and ways to improve their teaching practices, plan ways to involve families, and identify next steps.

References

Bishop-Josef, S.J., & E. Zigler. 2011. "The Cognitive/Academic Emphasis Versus the Whole Child Approach: The 50-Year Debate." Chap. 15 in *The Pre-K Debates: Current Controversies and Issues*, ed. E. Zigler, W.S. Gilliam, & W.S. Barnett, 83–88. Baltimore, MD: Brookes.

Bloom, B.S. 1964. *Stability and Change in Human Characteristics*. New York: Wiley & Sons.

Chi, M.T.H. 2009. "Active-Constructive-Interactive: A Conceptual Framework for Differentiating Learning Activities." *Topics in Cognitive Science* (1) 1: 73–105.

Ferrara, K., K. Hirsh-Pasek, N.S. Newcombe, R.M. Golinkoff, & W.S. Lam. 2011. "Block Talk: Spatial Language During Block Play." *Mind, Brain, & Education* (5) 3: 143–51.

Golinkoff, R.M., K. Hirsh-Pasek, S.W. Russ, & A.S. Lillard. 2013. "Guest Editors' Foreword. Probing Play: What Does the Research Show?" *American Journal of Play* (6) 1: xi–xii.

Gray, P. 2013. *Free to Learn: Why Unleashing the Instinct to Play Will Make Our Children Happier, More Self-Reliant, and Better Students for Life*. New York: Basic Books.

Hirsh-Pasek, K., J. Zosh, R.M. Golinkoff, J. Gray, M. Robb, & J. Kaufman. Forthcoming. "Harnessing the Science Of Learning To Promote Real Educational Apps." *Psychological Science in the Public Interest.*

Kagan, S.L., & A.E. Lowenstein. 2004. "School Readiness and Children's Play: Contemporary Oxymoron or Compatible Option?" In *Children's Play: The Roots of Reading*, ed. E.F. Zigler, D.G. Singer, & S.J. Bishop-Josef, 59–76. Washington, DC: ZERO TO THREE.

Lillard, A.S. 2013. "Playful Learning and Montessori Education." *American Journal of Play* 5 (2): 157–86.

Lillard, A.S., M.D. Lerner, E.J. Hopkins, R.A. Dore, E.D. Smith, & C.M. Palmquist. 2013. "The Impact of Pretend Play on Children's Development: A Review of the Evidence." *Psychological Bulletin* 139 (1): 1–34.

Zigler, E., & S.J. Bishop-Josef. 2009. "Play Under Siege: A Historical Overview." *Zero to Three* 30 (1): 4–11.

Zigler, E., W.S. Gilliam, & W.S. Barnett. 2011. *The Pre-K Debates: Current Controversies and Issues*. Baltimore, MD: Brookes.

Trudi Schwarz
and Julia
Luckenbill

Let's Get Messy! Learning Through Art and Sensory Play

It's raining lightly in the infant yard, where the babies are examining the wet grass and splashing in puddles. Aziz (17 months) picks up a ball and tosses it into a muddy puddle. He squeals in delight, bends down, and lifts the ball back up. He touches the mud, watching as it oozes onto his finger. He then drops the ball back into the puddle. Next, he walks over to a nearby shelf and grasps another ball, walks back, then drops that one into the puddle as well.

Fascinated by his messy discovery, Aziz continues to drop balls and other toys into the muddy water until it is time to go inside. Meanwhile, several other infants wobble over and imitate the game. Having observed the infants' interest, the next day the staff place a tub of water and balls in the indoor art and sensory area to extend the children's investigation.

Visitors to our classrooms who observe scenarios like the one described above often make surprised comments, such as "You let them get that messy?" But these projects are commonplace in our infant and toddler classrooms. As infant and toddler teachers we take a child-centered, emergent approach, meaning that we observe the children at play, ask ourselves what they are interested in learning, and design developmentally appropriate curricula to meet and extend those interests. This curriculum development technique leads the children to develop deeper understandings of how the world works. The activities in our classroom interest areas and our play yards change weekly, though

naeyc® 2, 3

> ### When We Talk About "Art"
>
> When we use the term *art* in this context, we are discussing activities that result in finished products, such as a painting on paper. The term *sensory* in this context refers to activities with no end product, such as running hands through a bin of birdseed. Art projects are sensory based, and sensory projects could be considered art. For this article, we use the terms interchangeably.

the interest areas remain in the same locations. When children arrive in the morning, they tend to beeline to their favorite areas to see what has changed. One of the preferred areas inside and outside is the art and sensory area.

We believe that art and sensory projects are integral to the curriculum, and that children develop key skills through these types of activities. This belief is supported by the Infant/Toddler Environment Rating Scale—Revised (Harms, Cryer, & Clifford 2007). We provide art and sensory activities every day and give children ample time to explore them. Why? As Mayesky (2015) says, the arts benefit children in myriad ways, including fostering creativity. She notes that "the unstructured quality of well-designed arts activities allows children to experiment with their voices, bodies, and familiar materials in new ways" (9). Through hands-on play, even infants are developing rudimentary theories (schemas) to explain their world. In other words, infants construct an idea of how things work in their heads, and then refine it over time through experience. For example, giving infants time to paint leads to them discovering that they have made marks on the paper. Over time, this understanding becomes more systematic and the children become capable of integrating new tools and media into their art.

Trudi Schwarz, MS, is the infant room lead teacher at the University of California–Davis Center for Child and Family Studies' NAEYC-accredited Early Childhood Lab School. She has presented at California AEYC and local early childhood education conferences. Her professional interests include infant language development and creating innovative infant curricula.

Julia Luckenbill, MA, is the infant and toddler program coordinator for the Early Childhood Lab School at UC-Davis. She has directed several preschool programs in California and presents on a range of child development topics for parents, teachers, and students. Her interests include sensory activities and integrating Reggio Emilia philosophy into US schools.

Learning and Growing Through Art and Sensory Play

Children benefit from engaging in hands-on exploration of materials. They add many vital "tools" to their school readiness toolbox through art and sensory play.

Motor Skill Development

- Poking, smashing, pinching, squeezing, cutting, and rolling playdough and real clay improves hand strength and fine motor skills.
- Grasping a crayon or marker and scribbling supports later writing and drawing skills. Toddlers initially use their whole arms to make scribble marks on paper. With practice they refine these skills and begin to make vague shapes. These early experiences enable children to plan their artwork and draw things that exist in their world when they reach preschool age.

Social-Emotional Skills

Engaging in art and sensory play supports the emergence of children's new social and emotional skills. For example,

- Painting with each other on a see-through easel or a shared piece of paper encourages children's ability to use materials together and supports prosocial interactions.

- Splashing side by side at the water table teaches toddlers about sharing spaces and leads to conversations about other children's feelings (e.g., if a child did not want to get wet).

Observing children's play provides teachers with vital information about children's developmental progress.

Brain Development

As Shabazian and Soga (2014) point out, "infants and toddlers need to play with objects that stimulate and enhance brain development" by having access to open-ended materials, which "do not have predetermined puposes but instead offer many possibilities" (61). Art materials are inherently open ended. We put them within reach of all the infants and toddlers, and the children use them as they please. According to Shabazian and Soga, this type of play helps young children develop divergent thinking, which they define as "the ability to view a problem from different perspectives" (62). Divergent thinking, these authors note, is an important step in developing problem-solving skills.

In this article, we share the experiences of the infant and toddler art and sensory program at our school. We begin with issues to consider when planning the curriculum and provide ideas about where to find inexpensive, high-quality materials. Finally, we share some examples from our classrooms and offer suggestions for yours.

Through hands-on play, even infants are developing rudimentary theories (schemas) to explain their world.

Planning a Curriculum

Visitors to our youngest classrooms are often surprised to discover that we have daily art and sensory activities, just as preschool classrooms do. However, there are essential differences between planning art and sensory activities for preschoolers and activities for infants and toddlers. Following are some things to consider when planning art and sensory activities.

Encourage Experimentation

Open-ended activities allow children the time and space they need to construct their own understanding of the materials and their properties. Infants enjoy using their senses to learn and are very oral, so it's best to design activities with this in mind. They love to gradually explore the texture, scent, taste, sight, and sound of the art materials. They often are messy in their use of the materials (e.g., crawling through paint). Materials must be washable and nontoxic and contain no small parts. Provide ample time for play and for cleanup.

Open-ended activities allow children the time and space they need to construct their own understanding of the materials and their properties.

Some adults are concerned that infants and young toddlers might eat the art materials. While we don't encourage this behavior, we understand that tasting the materials is part of the children's exploratory process. We have found that after a small sample, children realize that the materials are not tasty, and teachers can then redirect them to a more appropriate use. For example, after an infant puts a (nontoxic) paint-covered finger in his mouth, a teacher might say, "That doesn't taste so good. You can rub the paint on the paper instead." If you find that infants are eating large amounts of homemade playdough, switch to commercially made playdough or salt-free recipes, because an excess of salt is harmful to young children.

Supervise Exploration

As infants become toddlers, they use materials with more intentionality. They are less likely to eat the art materials, though they may still experiment by tasting them. Toddlers do not understand conservation of volume. They will squeeze a glue bottle until it is empty or shake all the colored sand out of the salt shaker and then demand more. They explore the nature of paint by decorating not only the paper, but also the table and themselves. Toddlers' explorations require close supervision from teachers and enough space to be messy.

Affirm the Process

Infants and toddlers are *process* rather than *product* oriented. Finger painting is more satisfying to them, and allows for greater exploration and experimentation, than placing cotton balls on the back of a die-cut sheep. Playing with playdough is more exciting and creative than coloring in a coloring book. Infants and toddlers want to feel the paint as it covers their fingers, smell the mint in the scented playdough, and taste the basil leaves in the tub on the table. As Mayesky (2015) notes, "The teacher's observation of the process that leads to originality (exploration and experimentation with the materials) is more valuable than any judgment of the product" (8).

Use Culturally Diverse Materials

Implement an antibias approach to all projects. Materials that reflect the cultures and backgrounds of the children you serve send a message that everyone is valued in the classroom (Derman-Sparks & Edwards 2010). For example, offer brown and tan playdough as well as pink shades, and training chopsticks to explore the playdough instead of plastic knives. Ask the children's parents to donate materials that reflect their backgrounds, such as origami or wrapping paper for use in collage. The more you keep the families in mind, the more inclusive and welcoming your program will be.

A Note on Cultural Sensitivity

Some cultures consider it offensive to use food as an art material—in particular, rice. Avoid this kind of activity, as you cannot be sure who may be offended by the waste of food. It is not always obvious if a child or their extended family have experienced food scarcity (Derman-Sparks & Edwards 2010). We have found that birdseed is a good nontoxic alternative to rice in a sensory table, and that fish tank gravel and cornstarch-based packing peanuts (they melt in your mouth) work just as well as beans and pasta for gluing on collages.

Make Accommodations for Special Needs

Art and sensory projects must be accessible to all children in your program and address a range of skills and abilities. This may mean making accommodations for children with special needs. For instance, you can place materials directly on the floor for children with mobility challenges or for those who cannot stand at a table. You can provide paintbrushes with extra-large handles for children with fine motor difficulty. To create them, wind self-adhering first aid tape around the handle of the brush to make it easier to grasp.

Modify Activities for Sensory Avoiders

Differences in temperament impact each child's response to art and sensory materials. For example, some children love the feel of gooey wet paint on their hands, while other children shy away from such slimy activities. If you have children in your program who avoid sensory experiences, you can include them by modifying sticky and gooey projects. For example, add brushes in the finger paint or cups with oobleck (a cornstarch and water mixture) so these children can explore the materials at their own pace and in a way that feels right to them. When sensory-avoidant children are exposed to art materials in a way that respects their unique temperaments, they may become more comfortable touching the materials as they become familiar with textures. Playing with finger paint, bubble water, and other sensory materials is part of a healthy "sensory diet" for all children. Engaging in these activities can help a child with sensory processing disorder (and children without the disorder as well) more easily interpret the environment (Arnwine 2007, 4).

Display Children's Artwork

Display the children's artwork at their eye level. This allows them to admire their creations and feel ownership of the classroom. Families also appreciate seeing their children's creations valued. Display 3-D art, such as playdough sculptures, in addition to paper collages and paintings. Children's art displays are an indicator of a high-quality classroom in the NAEYC accreditation standards and in both the Infant/Toddler and the Early Childhood Environment Rating Scale—Revised (ITERS-R/ECERS-R), which are tools used to assess the quality of early childhood learning environments (Harms, Clifford, & Cryer 2005; Harms, Cryer, & Clifford 2007).

Art and Sensory Activities in the Infant Room

It is wise to plan activities for young children in order to avoid chaotic transitions. When teachers plan curriculum based on their observations of children's interests, children's learning experiences are extended. Below is an example from our infant room.

Choosing the Activity

At snack time, we noticed 11-month-old Alice smearing her sweet potato on the table and gazing intently at the color. Other infants were also smearing their food while eating. Since the infants were clearly interested in spreading color, we decided that finger paint was a good extension.

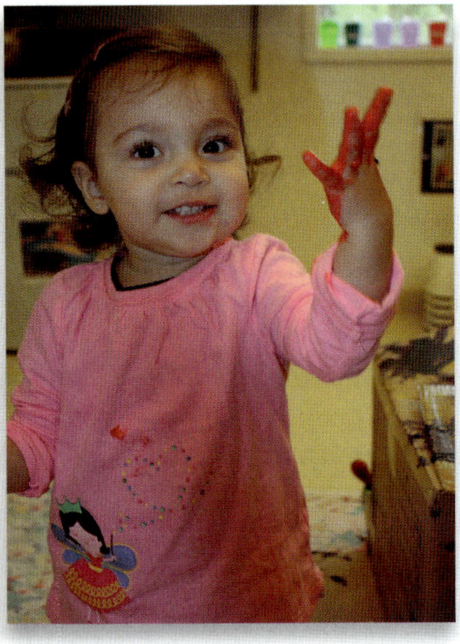

Designing the Activity

We decided to introduce nontoxic foam paint in the art and sensory area. We placed the paint in a low bin on the floor and put wipes on a table near the paint.

Implementing the Activity

On the first day, several infants crawled or wobbled over to the paint bin. Some reached in, grasping and smearing the paint. Others poked it lightly with a finger or avoided it. We continued for several days, with adults modeling that it was safe to touch the paint. Over the course of the week we saw more infants join in.

Changing the Activity

In response to the children's initial reaction to the project, we planned the following extensions:

1. We added round-ended paintbrushes (like shaving brushes), inviting infants to engage with the paint without smearing their fingers. Teachers encouraged the children to explore the materials, and they modeled using the brushes without requiring infants to try them.
2. The following week, we observed the infants still showing interest in the paint. We changed the project very little, substituting finger paint for foam paint. The finger paint was more slippery than the foam paint. The infants continued to engage with the paint.
3. We noticed that when we washed the paint off the infants' hands, they enjoyed the bubbles and water. We changed the paint to soapy water. More infants joined in this exploration—splashing, dumping items in the water, and even crawling in. The children engaged in this activity outside as well as inside.

Some children love the feel of gooey wet paint on their hands, while other children shy away from such slimy activities.

Sensory and Art Activities for Infants and Toddlers

Nontoxic material	Nontoxic items to place on or in the material	Surface	Tools	Ages and notes
Tempera paint, foam paint, finger paint	Colored sand and liquid soap	Paper, Plexiglass, wood, cardboard items, natural items, body parts, bubble wrap	Paintbrushes, stamps, sponges, plastic cars, plastic balls	Infants and toddlers
Watercolor block paint or liquid paint	None	Paper, coffee filters	Water, brushes, bottles for liquid watercolor	Toddlers
Contact paper	Colored sand, regular sand, natural materials, paper scraps, pictures from magazines, photos, recycled wrapping paper, pipe cleaners, tissue paper	Table or floor	Scotch tape or similar to affix contact paper to the table	Infants and toddlers
Stickers, tape	None	Paper or skin	None	Infants and toddlers
Construction paper, cardboard, tissue paper, newspaper, butcher paper, etc.	None	Table or floor	Tape to affix to the paper or materials to decorate it	Infants and toddlers. Crumpling, tearing, climbing into containers of crumpled paper, and making balls of paper.
Glue	None	Table with trays and paper or cardboard to hold collage	Glue bottles	Toddlers
Playdough, purchased or homemade. (*Note:* Limit how much playdough children eat due to the high salt content, or make salt-free playdough, or purchase commercial playdough.)	Colored sand; liquid watercolor, food color, or extract (e.g., vanilla or peppermint); pipe cleaners; Popsicle sticks; leaves, sticks, shells, etc.	Table with trays to define each child's space, or a bin if a group of infants shares the playdough	Cookie cutters, cutting tools, baking tools, ceramic tools, tortilla presses, garlic presses, plastic toys as props	Infants and toddlers
Natural clay	Pipe cleaners, Popsicle sticks, nontoxic branches, water if clay is dry	Table or bin, trays optional	See above	Infants and toddlers. Clean up well after using clay to prevent dust buildup.
Water	Liquid watercolor or food color, soap, large ice blocks (but remove when they become smaller), cornstarch mixture (oobleck), wool	Bins on or off a table. Towels taped to floor around this project.	Cups, funnels, bath toys, measuring cups, whisks, items that sink and float, eyedroppers for toddlers	Infants and toddlers
Birdseed, sand, soil	Hidden toys or shells under the material. Water in the sand or soil.	Bins inside or outside to decrease mess. Water table.	Containers, sand mills, plastic vehicles or animals, various sizes of tubes, plastic beakers	Infants and toddlers
Nontoxic leaves, pinecones, seedpods, flowers	Water, soil, clay	Table, bin, piles outside	Scissors (for toddlers only)	Infants and toddlers
Stamping ink/dot markers	None	Table with individual papers or butcher paper if this is a communal artwork. Wall with butcher paper.	Stamps for stamp pad. Both age groups are more likely to use hands.	Infants and toddlers
Crayons, colored pencils, markers, nontoxic oil pastels, chalk	None	Table with individual papers or butcher paper if this is a communal artwork. Wall with butcher paper.	None	Older infants and toddlers. Use chalk outside or with ventilation to prevent dust buildup.
Fabric	None	Can be connected into a "sensory blanket" with other materials such as bubble wrap for young infants to crawl over. Older children can use it on a table for collage.	Scissors (for toddlers only)	Infants and toddlers. Invites open-ended dramatic play and dance for toddlers.

Sources for Art and Sensory Materials

Materials available commercially: Tempera paint, foam paint, watercolor paint, glue, Popsicle sticks, colored sand, paper, contact paper, tape, stamp pads and stamps, birdseed, feathers, soap, sponges.

Materials found at thrift stores: Cups and funnels, magazines for clipping images for collage, and kitchen utensils.

Nontoxic natural materials (bleach them before children put them in their mouths, using the ratio of bleach to water recommended by applicable regulations and licensing protocol): Straw, non-toxic leaves and seeds, flowers and sticks, wool, shells, rocks, gourds, pinecones, sand, mud.

Using these materials is beneficial to young children—handling nontoxic pinecones and leaves in a bin encourages a love of nature and engages all of a child's senses (White & Stoecklin 2008).

Materials found in the home or classroom: Paper towel rolls, yogurt containers, plastic water bottles, recycled paper, newspaper, cardboard boxes of all sizes, egg cartons, canning jar lids, water, old towels to make rags.

Materials created from scratch: Playdough, finger paint, oobleck, "clean mud," colored salt/sand. There are many recipes for these online and in the library.

4. We decided to explore oobleck. Oobleck looks a lot like paint and contains water and cornstarch, but it behaves differently than these substances. The infants were initially hesitant around this substance. They gradually joined in, especially after plastic cups were introduced so they could examine the substance without touching it, if they preferred.

Making a Record

To share the children's explorations with families and the wider community, we documented each infant art and sensory activity in our classroom photo essay, "Adventures in the Infant Room." The photo essays help parents and teachers look back on infant and toddler learning. They also help capture the range of process-based activities and model how they might be tried at home. Here is an excerpt from the infant room's oobleck documentation:

Julia is observing Leo (15 months) and the oobleck. She has noticed that he avoids touching many sensory materials, using towels, cups, or brushes to engage with them instead. She locates cups as Leo joins the activity. Next she observes Leo touching the cups. She knows that he likes to enter play slowly.

Julia notes Leo's gaze shifting from the cup to the oobleck. He lightly touches the oobleck. His finger comes back clean but wet. She responds by using parallel talk, a teaching technique in which teachers describe aloud what children are doing in order to connect with them and expand their ideas. Julia says, "You touched it and now your finger is wet. Oobleck is wet." She imitates his action. Leo pushes his cup back into the oobleck, bottom first. Julia says, "If you want to pick up the oobleck, you can use the cup." She models this by filling her own cup with oobleck. She pours the oobleck out. "It comes out slowly," she comments. "Do you want to try?" Leo reaches out and grasps her cup and pours out the oobleck.

The oobleck falls in puddles. Leo now appears comfortable with the substance. He grasps handfuls of it, pinches and squeezes it, and puts it back into his cup. Julia, still observing him, continues to facilitate his play, moving the oobleck back into the cups for further pouring. She narrates the action of the oobleck—how slowly it moves—and she talks about how Leo can pinch it to pick it up. She also steps back again, allowing him to feel autonomous in his exploration.

Families and Play

Here are some suggestions for talking with families about play.

- Point out the variety of skills and knowledge children gain when they play. For example, as they interact with each other and with materials, children learn how to get along with their peers, manage their emotions in an appropriate way, and develop cognitive, language, and motor skills.
- Describe some games and activities that the children participate in at the program and what they learn from them. For example, in the block area children learn how to share materials, collaborate with peers, and plan and design structures. They also develop fine motor control.
- Explain that skills learned during play form the foundation for learning academics. For example, children need self-regulation, including the ability to sustain attention and control their anger or frustration, as they learn to read and understand cognitive concepts. The fine motor skills they develop while playing with small toys such as Legos will help them learn to hold and write with a pencil.
- Remind families that play is not just for the young! Encourage them to get everyone involved in play, including grandparents and other extended family members. This reinforces family connections and creates positive memories.
- Share examples of inexpensive toys to make and play with. A simple cardboard box, a few pieces of sidewalk chalk, or blanket and chairs to make a hideaway all inspire children's imagination and can provide hours of fun, social engagement, and learning.
- Emphasize that all types of play are valuable for young children, including solitary play and safe rough-and-tumble play (supervised and within reasonable limits). (See pp. 107–117 in this volume.) Outdoor play is particularly beneficial, as it helps children learn to appreciate nature and often has a soothing effect on children who are agitated. In addition, active play is critical for developing bodies and minds. Encourage families to do activities with their children that involve their whole bodies, such as a game of tag.
- Encourage families to talk to children about their play. This stimulates vocabulary development and lets children know that the adults in their lives value what they are doing.
- Explain that word play is as important—and fun—as other types of play. Encourage families to sing with their children and play games like "I spy" and rhyming and number games. Riding in a vehicle is a great time to do these activities.
- Offer sources and research that support the importance of play in supporting children's learning. Some excellent websites for families to investigate are the Center on the Social and Emotional Foundations for Early Learning (http://csefel.vanderbilt.edu), Zero to Three (www.zerotothree.org), and NAEYC's For Families (families.naeyc.org).

Art and Sensory Activities in the Toddler Room

We use the same techniques to design and expand curriculum in both the infant and toddler programs. Following is an example of a curriculum designed for older children.

Choosing the Activity

Playdough was a passion in the toddler room. Each day children asked for it by name, and they crowded around as we placed the trays on the tables, reaching for playdough and tools. We provided cookie cutters, butter knives, pizza cutters, and rolling pins to use

with the dough. We noticed several toddlers putting globs of playdough on the butter knives and declaring them to be "Popsicles."

Designing and Implementing the Activity

We put out a range of materials, from Popsicle sticks and pipe cleaners to feathers and leaves, and then watched what the toddlers did and made. They excitedly created many "birthday cakes" by poking items into the playdough. They enjoyed singing "Happy Birthday" to themselves, their peers, and their teachers.

Changing the Activity

In response to the children's initial reaction to the project, we planned the following extensions:

1. Noting the toddlers' interest in cakes, we set up a bakery shop. We added brown playdough, birthday candles, whisks, measuring cups, cupcake tins and wrappers, salt-filled shakers, and other baking tools to the trays. The toddlers jumped right in, making more cakes and cupcakes. They were particularly interested in the salt shakers and sometimes got into conflicts over taking turns using them, which offered opportunities to help the children practice problem solving.
2. We decided to make salt shaker art. We filled small glue bottles with about a tablespoon of glue apiece. We placed construction paper on trays, anticipating glue puddles. We placed colored sand in several recycled spice shakers and taped over some of the holes to make the sand come out slowly. The toddlers made small glue lakes and shook all the sand out into colorful piles. We scooped the excess sand up, refilled the spice containers, and repeated the process. The toddlers did not understand that the glue made the sand stick, or that if they used too much glue the sand would fall off, but they loved the process. As expected, this was a developmentally appropriate outcome. Although children at this age do not carefully use glue, they do enjoy the experience of emptying, squeezing, and making a mess.
3. We added food coloring to the glue in the bottles after observing that the toddlers enjoyed using the glue puddles as paint.
4. The toddlers did not want to stop using shakers—it was so much fun! We took the activity outside to the dramatic play table beside the sandbox. Here the toddlers could make a mess using filled shakers without getting the classroom salty or sandy. They could also refill the shakers with sand. We knew the toddlers would "ruin" the playdough with the sand, but we accepted this as part of the process. This project included the initial playdough and accessories, salt shakers filled with various substances, and glue with and without food color.

Memo to: Infant and Toddler Teachers Everywhere
From: Linda Gillespie and Rebecca Parlakian
Date: January 2015
Subject: Play—The True Work of Childhood

Play is often referred to as a child's work. As infant and toddler teachers know well, play is a profoundly important medium for learning and development for very young children. Beginning at birth, play unfolds in the context of a responsive, caring adult—that's you—who sets the stage for exploration by creating a safe base from which babies can explore. Through playful back-and-forth interaction with their important adults, including both family members and teachers, babies learn they are loved, important, and fun to be with. Discoveries made by infants and toddlers lay the foundation for critical social-emotional qualities such as self-confidence, self-esteem, a sense of identity, and the desire to relate to and connect with others—including their peers and favorite adults (like you and your colleagues). Children use these early social-emotional skills to establish and maintain reciprocal relationships all their lives.

Within a loving and supportive relationship, baby's play unfolds. During play, babies lift, drop, look, pour, bounce, hide, build, knock down, and more. They test key scientific concepts, such as the sounds various objects make when tossed off a high chair tray, and discover the function of objects (to roll, to pop up, or to be stacked). Between birth and age 3, children are developing mathematical concepts, including the concepts *all gone*, *more*, and *less*, and the meaning of *one* and *two*. Spatially, babies are experimenting by using shape sorters, nesting cups, and stacking blocks, and trying to fit their bodies into various spaces. They master language and literacy skills as they learn the sounds of their parents' and teachers' voices, discover the rules of conversation, and act out stories in dramatic play. All this learning during play is because you and other important adults take the time to respond, set up the environment, plan, and carefully observe babies' play.

Play is, indeed, the true work of childhood. When we observe carefully, it tells us what children know and what they are thinking about; what they are wondering, testing, and predicting; and, most important, what skills they are ready to master. And then we, as caring teachers, can plan and support their development and learning. Play is a joyful process of testing, learning, and discovery within supportive relationships with parents, teachers, providers, and peers. Play offers a path through which infants and toddlers gain the skills, knowledge, and joy in learning that prove essential to success in school and beyond.

Linda Gillespie, MS, at ZERO TO THREE, focuses on babies and families, and **Rebecca Parlakian,** MA, promotes the healthy development of infants and toddlers as director of parenting resources at ZERO TO THREE.

Making a Record

To share the children's explorations with parents and visitors to our school, we documented each toddler art and sensory activity in the classroom in a photo essay, "Adventures in the Toddler Room." Here is an excerpt from the toddler room's glue-and-sand activity:

> We introduced glue-and-sand painting. This was a direct extension of last week's bakery shop project. We noticed that the toddlers loved using shakers and enjoyed decorating with sand.
>
> Peter is using both hands to squeeze out colored glue from the bottle. He has placed his sand down before the glue. This shows us that he does not understand that the glue will make the sand stick to the paper, but that he is testing out the properties of both materials on the paper.
>
> Andy and Joo are engaging in a similar process, testing the materials without being told how to use them by an adult. They are developing strong fine motor skills as they handle the tools.

Conclusion

We have found that the art and sensory experiences in the infant and toddler classrooms are some of the most exciting that we provide. Well-planned projects that include time for exploration and a way to control—or at least contain—the mess allow everyone to relax and enjoy the process. We encourage you to try art and sensory activities with the infants and toddlers in your program. There is nothing like seeing a child realize that she has caused a mark on a paper, or watching a toddler discover for himself that mixing blue and red makes purple. While art explorations with infants and toddlers are certainly more work for teachers, they have a strong positive impact on young children's development and learning.

References

Arnwine, B. 2007. *Starting Sensory Integration Therapy: Fun Activities That Won't Destroy Your Home or Classroom.* Arlington, TX: Future Horizons.

Derman-Sparks, L., & J.O. Edwards. 2010. *Anti-Bias Education for Young Children and Ourselves.* Washington, DC: NAEYC.

Harms, T., R.M. Clifford, & D. Cryer. 2005. *Early Childhood Environment Rating Scale Revised.* New York: Teachers College Press.

Harms, T., D. Cryer, & R.M. Clifford. 2007. *Infant/Toddler Environment Rating Scale Revised Edition.* New York: Teachers College Press.

Mayesky, M. 2015. *Creative Activities and Curriculum for Young Children.* 11th ed. Stamford, CT: Cengage Learning.

Shabazian, A.N., & C.L. Soga. 2014. "Making the Right Choice Simple: Selecting Materials for Infants and Toddlers." *Young Children* (69) 3: 60–65.

White, R., & V.L. Stoecklin. 2008. "Nurturing Children's Biophilia: Developmentally Appropriate Environmental Education for Young Children." *Collage: Resources for Early Childhood Educators,* Nov. www.whitehutchinson.com/children/articles/nurturing.shtml.

Deb Curtis, Kasondra L. Brown, Lorrie Baird, and Anne Marie Coughlin

Lively Minds at Play: Planning Environments and Materials That Support the Way Young Children Learn

During our many years working as teachers of young children, teacher educators, and colleagues offering professional activities together as Harvest Resources associates (www.ecetrainers.com), we have come to admire toddlers' avid curiosity, determination, bigheartedness, and delight in engaging with people and the world around them. From our review of current research about the learning capacities of children under age 3, we realize that the eagerness toddlers have for almost every encounter is no accident, and we have taken it upon ourselves to study more about them.

Research confirms that during the toddler years children experience one of the most significant periods of development and learning. Children under age 3 have exceptionally flexible brains that allow them to hear more, see more, and experience more than adults. Their enhanced learning abilities reflect special features in their brains that make them more conscious than adults. They also innately approach learning in the same way scientists do, using the scientific method to experiment and analyze the results of what they discover. When toddlers use their brains well, through focused, sustained activity, their potential is enormous (Gopnik 2009).

Some Materials Limit Exploration

Many times, the environments and materials offered to toddlers emphasize health and safety. While health and safety are important, an overemphasis on these features can limit the possibilities for richer experiences of exploration, collaboration, and learning. Some commonly used materials provide few opportunities that engage children in the complex ways their lively minds deserve. Most toys chosen for use in child care settings have hard, plastic, unyielding surfaces that adults can easily sanitize. Toddler toys frequently teach simple concepts like color and shape or have a cause-and-effect component, such as a button or knob that beeps or lights up. Children might accidentally discover this feature or adults show them what it does. Once children figure out the minimal uses for these objects, there is not much else to challenge their lively minds.

Implied in the use of such materials may be the view of some educators that toddlers have limited capabilities or inner resources and require overstimulating experiences to stay interested in an activity or toy. Instead, what if we recognize and provide for toddlers' dynamic brains and their capacity for seeing and using materials in boundless ways? What if, rather than thinking of materials as a way to teach or entertain toddlers, we are eager to see the extraordinary discoveries they make?

There is much for us to learn about translating research into practices for offering out-of-the-ordinary materials to toddlers. We strongly support the health, safety, and well-being of all children, but in this article, we want to discuss providing children with fascinating materials and supervised experiences that engage and challenge them. We have found that when teachers recognize the profound nature of toddlers' learning abilities, they are excited to provide supervised experiences with interesting and challenging open-ended materials. They more willingly tackle the barriers and worries that come with health and safety standards, as well as overcome the reluctance to offer messy experiences that take extra effort to clean up. And they come to join in the delight and discovery with children.

Deb Curtis, MA, a teacher of adults and children, has coauthored several books for early childhood educators, including *Designs for Living and Learning: Transforming Early Childhood Environments* (Redleaf Press).

Kasondra L. Brown, BS, is a consultant and trainer with Collaborative for Children–United Way Bright Beginnings in Houston, Texas. Kasondra serves as a coach, mentor, and college instructor.

Lorrie Baird, RECE (registered early childhood educator), is the associate executive director of Kawartha Child Care Services in Peterborough, Ontario. She has been a teacher, program director, and college faculty member.

Anne Marie Coughlin, ECEC (early childhood educator and certified), RECE, is program director for London Bridge Child Care Services in London, Ontario, and provincial director for the Canadian Association for Young Children. She is an associate with Harvest Resources.

The authors would like to thank teachers Lauren Forcier and Lachana Fisher, who contributed notes about children engaged in schema play.

Toddlers and Sensory Materials

Toddlers' explorations of materials are filled with small actions during which they hear and see more than adults do. Because adults experience the world so differently (Gopnik 2009), seeing the significance of what toddlers are doing requires that we stop to notice the details of their actions and try to imagine what they might be thinking. To help cultivate our ability to see children's minds at work, we offered a collection of natural materials—including shells, wood rounds, and stones in wooden bowls—to a group of toddlers. We placed the materials on fabric and placemats to create a visual focus for the children. The materials gave the toddlers many possibilities for investigating texture, shape, color, size, weight, light, and sound. The toddlers manipulated the materials by dumping, filling, and transporting them. We carefully planned this experience, making sure we were with the toddlers for the entire activity to supervise for safety.

A Lively Mind at Work

As we observed 19-month-old Javier, and later studied the photos of his explorations, we saw evidence of his flexible, scientific brain at work. Javier eagerly approached the

materials, placing his entire hand inside a wooden bowl filled with stones, shells, and wood rounds. He carefully studied each of the objects. He touched the variety of natural objects and moved them into piles, perhaps noticing the similarities and differences of the items. With a look of wonder, Javier closely examined the stones he held in his hands. Next he tapped two stones together. His actions resulted in clicking sounds. Javier began to immerse himself in the materials as he placed objects on his head. He slid the stones down his face and dropped them back into the bowl.

Next Javier put an insect specimen encased in acrylic up to his eyes. We wondered if he was exploring its transparent and magnifying properties. Then Javier put the specimen block to his mouth and moved it around his lips, tongue, and teeth, perhaps exploring the texture, taste, and temperature that his other senses did not pick up.

Throughout this experience, Javier used all five senses and explored the materials in ways we never would have imagined. He seemed to have a purpose or question for every action he tried. We took his smallest actions seriously, and were impressed with his deep engagement with these objects. This motivated us to offer more possibilities for him to use his abilities to explore and learn.

Calling on Toddlers' Aesthetic Sense

Javier's meaningful engagement in exploring these materials moved us to expand our definition of sensory experiences, like water play and sand play, to include aesthetics. *Webster's Dictionary* suggests that *aesthetic* comes from a Greek word meaning *perception*. Aesthetic development is a focused way of knowing and experiencing the world that involves engaging with the senses. Feelings, processes, and responses to objects and experiences are heightened, leading to an appreciation of the beauty found in the world and allowing us to become totally lost in the moment (Curtis & Carter 2008). This definition fit Javier's investigations perfectly. Toddlers' senses are highly attuned to taking in the sights, sounds, and movements that surround them. Why not take advantage of their enhanced abilities and design our environments to create more and varied opportunities for seeing and discovering the world? With toddlers' aesthetic senses in mind, we now regularly add pleasing elements to our learning environments and find that the children engage with them enthusiastically.

Seeing Schemas

As we continued to observe the details of children's investigations with interesting materials, we saw more evidence of their active brains at work and we identified examples of actions related to other learning theories. The following observation is an example of children exploring schemas as identified by child psychologist Jean Piaget. A *schema* is a line of thought that is demonstrated by repeated actions and patterns in children's play. These repeated actions suggest that this play is a reflection of inner and specifically directed thoughts. When children explore schemas, they are building on their understanding of abstract ideas, patterns, and concepts (van Wijk 2008). Here are some of the schemas Piaget identified as applied to a toddler (Piaget & Inhelder [1969] 2000):

- **Transporting**—Picks things up, moves things, puts things down, or dumps.
- **Transforming**—Uses materials to explore changes in shape, color, consistency, and such.
- **Trajectory**—Explores the horizontal, vertical, and diagonal movement of things and herself. Makes things fly through the air, moves her own body in these ways.
- **Rotation and circulation**—Experiments with things that turn, such as wheels and balls; explores curved lines and circles.

- **Enclosing and enveloping**—Surrounds objects with other things. Moves himself inside a defined area, like a ring of blocks or a box. Hides, covers, or wraps himself and other things.
- **Connecting**—Joins things together and ties things up.
- **Disconnecting**—Takes things apart, scatters pieces and parts (van Wijk 2008).

We offered the children a variety of materials, including balls, ramps, trays, and containers, to invite their investigation of schemas. The materials, although common, were not something we had offered to them before in this combination. Would the children be interested in these items? Would the small objects be safe for the children to use? Would the children throw the balls around wildly? Our concerns were quickly put to rest when we witnessed the competence and focus the children brought to this experience.

The children walked into the room with confidence and quickly made their way to the carpet where we had set up the materials for play. Without directions or ideas from the adults, they discovered a multitude of possibilities the simple materials offered. For nearly an hour the children explored in the following ways:

Families and Play

Families are eager to hear about what their children are learning. To help families understand the value of play with open-ended materials, use photos and notes to share stories of their children's activities and discoveries. Discuss these items at drop-off and pickup times, send them home, or include them in a portfolio or at a parent conference. Create documentation displays in your classroom or hallway, with notes about what children are learning through their play experiences.

Invite families to join you in watching their children as they play, if even for a few minutes. Discuss what you notice:

- What seems to interest children about the materials they're exploring—textures, shapes, colors, weight, sizes, or ways they can combine them
- How the materials support the children's focus and purposeful learning
- What ideas the children might be investigating and what discoveries they might be making

Families are often thrilled to learn about inexpensive materials they can provide at home that will facilitate their children's learning. Send home a bag of open-ended materials or a list of ideas for using them, such as the following. Include the questions below for parents to consider as they watch their children play.

Fur and Fabric

Offer a variety of fake fur pieces and fabric with different colors and textures, such as soft and shaggy materials and interesting animal prints. If possible, provide stuffed animals that match the prints and fur pieces. Include some brushes for your child to use with the fur.

Tubes and Balls

Collect clear plastic and hard cardboard tubes of varying widths and lengths. Give your child different kinds and sizes of balls to explore with the tubes—craft, cotton, table tennis, golf, tennis, and so on. Add containers with lids for your child to put balls in and watch them roll out.

Items From Nature

Gather a variety of seashells, pinecones, rocks, gourds, and seed pods for your child to explore, along with boxes and baskets. Your child might use the containers to sort the items or hide them.

Coaster Sets

Coasters come in all shapes and sizes and often have matching boxes that the coasters fit into.

Napkin Rings

Napkin rings are great for stacking and rolling as well as stringing when paired with lengths of ribbon.

As your child plays with the materials, notice how she uses her senses to explore and learn about them. Your child might be thinking, "What does this look, feel, sound, smell, and taste like?"

Notice how your child tries to discover how the objects work and what he can do with them. Your child might be thinking about questions like these:

- What can this do?
- What can I do with this?
- How do these things work together?
- How can I use this to connect with other people?

Imitate what you see your child doing to show her you that you see her ideas. Your attention tells your child that her actions have value and will encourage her to keep exploring and acting on her ideas.

Use new words and phrases to describe what you see your child doing and what he seems to be thinking. This will help build his vocabulary.

- Noticed and repeated the many ways they could make sounds with the materials
- Negotiated various ways to fill and dump the containers and tubes
- Used the ramps and tubes to transport balls and other objects to various places in the room and to send them to a friend or a teacher
- Balanced the balls to move them back and forth between the tubes
- Rolled the balls rapidly down the ramps, concentrating on balancing them to keep them from flying off the ramps
- Manipulated the balls so they were spinning around and around on the trays

Materials for Supervised Investigations

To enhance toddlers' incredible potential, we plan experiences and offer materials for children to use when pursuing their instinctive and extensive approaches to learning. The following are examples of materials we offer toddlers for their supervised investigations:

- A collection of mirrors, metal containers, bracelets, jewels, and jewelry holders gives children opportunities to explore enclosing and enveloping, as well as rotation and circularity (experimenting with how things turn and spin); the mirrors' reflections and the shiny objects appeal to children's aesthetic sense
- Textured tiles and shiny wooden wedges encourage children to connect and disconnect the items in rows and lines, possibly using shape, color, and size as references
- Bamboo cove molding, plastic troughs, and balls, spools, and other objects that roll invite children to explore trajectory in a focused way
- Colorful bracelets, round containers with lids, and paper towel holders provide children with opportunities to explore rotation and circularity
- Colored water in small containers, pipettes, and ice cube trays invite children to explore transforming and transporting as they change the color of the water and move it from the bowls to the pipettes and then into ice cube trays
- Gak and Flubber (homemade), along with a wire rack, intrigue children when they discover their ability to transform these magical substances

- Observed each other's ideas and actions and imitated what they saw one another doing
- Tested new ideas as they observed other children's actions, which caused their explorations to evolve, change, and grow more complicated

We were surprised when we realized that an hour had passed and the children remained immersed in the play. Our role was to observe their actions, narrate what we saw, and help them see each other's actions. We were also there to supervise safe use of the materials, but we were surprised to note that none of us had to intervene in this way.

While watching the toddlers play, we realized that their actions—including some we previously prohibited—had a significance we had never noticed before. For example, because we understood that making things move and fly is the trajectory schema, we found ways to support the children's work with the concept: when they threw the balls to watch them fly, we offered tubes, ramps, and dowels and challenged the children to control the movement with the props. When toddlers use their adaptable brains to explore, they are learning unlimited possibilities for how the world can be. They consider and act on countless unconventional ideas that can alarm or delight us. This is the gift young children bring to the world and to us. As they grow older they will put all they have discovered to use—to invent what has yet to be imagined or perhaps to solve the serious problems of our time (Gopnik 2009).

As toddlers grow older they will put all they have discovered to use.

Principles for Planning Environments and Choosing Materials

Through our observations, we developed principles that we turn to again and again as we strive to ensure that our practices engage children's capabilities (Curtis & Carter 2003).

Offer materials in careful combinations and collections. Find open-ended and unusual materials at unusual sources, such as garden stores, garage sales, or thrift stores. Here are some items to combine:

- Wooden trays, bowls, massage balls, spools
- Faux fur and fabric pieces with different colors and textures (soft, shaggy, sheer, shiny)
- Tubes, balls, and containers with lids
- Natural items, such as seashells, pinecones, rocks, gourds, dried flowers, twigs, and pods
- Coaster sets, napkin rings, hair curlers, paper towel tubes, and candle holders
- Light-reflecting and colorful objects (flashlights, color paddles, prisms, and other translucent, shiny objects)

Explore materials for their possibilities before offering them to children. This will help you see what the children may find engaging.

Display materials in an orderly, enticing way. Place them on a particular rug or mat to create a visual focus and to signify a time for play. Make sure the space and materials are accessible to all children. For children with special physical needs, stabilize materials with suction cups, grip liners, and/or Velcro. Children with visual impairments may need items presented in a high-contrast format.

Memo to: Early Childhood Program Directors
From: Mary Mackrain
Date: January 2015
Subject: Play Is Vital for Healthy Brains and Relationships

Play offers rich, daily experiences as children negotiate with peers, engage in make-believe, and discover the world around them. Participating in play can be thought of as lighting up the circuitry board of a computer, with children's experiences firing up neuron connections in their developing brains (Center on the Developing Child at Harvard University 2011). The prefrontal cortex, in conjunction with other parts of the brain, is where executive functioning takes place—enabling children to hone functions like self-regulation, attention, and problem solving. All of these are critical ingredients for learning throughout life.

Play also provides a natural learning environment for children to develop healthy, meaningful relationships. Young children are still working on the skills to solve conflicts, engage in productive back-and-forth with peers, and share an array of feelings in healthy ways. When adults offer gentle guidance and support in the course of children's play, children learn to negotiate the messy and sometimes unpredictable circumstances they face. Managing strong emotions, understanding others' emotions, and learning to trust and ask for help are valuable life skills formed through the interactions that play supports.

Directors can support teachers by ensuring sufficient resources to provide playful learning environments. In addition, encourage teachers to provide lots of play opportunities for the children in their classrooms. Doing so *now* will enable you and the teachers to give children the tools they need to talk about how they feel in safe ways, handle daily challenges, solve problems, and focus on important tasks—*forever*.

Reference

Center on the Developing Child at Harvard University. 2011. "Building the Brain's "Air Traffic Control" System: How Early Experiences Shape the Development of Executive Function." Working Paper No.11. http://www.developingchild.harvard.edu.

Mary Mackrain, MEd, IMH-E®, is an early childhood project director for Education Development Center in Waltham, Massachusetts.

Provide ample time and space for a small group (four or five children) to play with the materials. Don't hurry or offer ideas too soon. Some children may need more time to begin their investigations or to see more possibilities. It is best if children work at their own pace and learn from each other.

Sit nearby to supervise. Be sure to take an interest in what the children are doing as they work.

Offer descriptions and narrations of what you see unfolding. What you give attention to supports children's interests and communicates to them that their pursuits have value. Describing and narrating children's actions gives them an awareness that they have ideas they can use to explore the world. This in turn helps them develop self-regulation, initiative, and language. Narrating also helps you avoid dictating, controlling, or directing.

Observe children to learn their interests and points of view. Use these questions to guide your observations:

- What are the children drawn to about the materials—textures, shapes, colors, weight, size, or combinations?
- How do the materials support the children's focus and purposeful actions so they stay with a particular investigation for an hour or more?
- How do the children manipulate the materials to learn about them? What actions reflect the children's flexible brains and learning capabilities?
- What possible experiments and theories are the children working on?

Conclusion

When we offer meaningful materials to children and study the details of their actions to identify the significance they hold, we become intellectually engaged with children in their pursuits. We understand the role we play in providing vital materials and opportunities to explore and learn. Every day teachers witness complex learning and potential in the children they work with.

We invite you to offer a collection of unusual learning materials to toddlers. Notice the way they immerse themselves in the rich and magical world around them. Appreciate the flexible thinking and skills children use in their exploration and discovery. Share in the joy of being alert and alive. If we open ourselves to it, we learn from children to see and experience the world in new and wondrous ways!

References

Curtis, D., & M. Carter. 2003. *Designs for Living and Learning: Transforming Early Childhood Environments*. St. Paul, MN: Redleaf.

Curtis, D., & M. Carter. 2008. *Learning Together With Young Children: A Curriculum Framework for Reflective Teachers*. St. Paul, MN: Redleaf.

Gopnik, A. 2009. *The Philosophical Baby: What Children's Minds Tell Us About Truth, Love, and the Meaning of Life*. New York: Farrar, Straus, & Giroux.

Piaget, J., & B. Inhelder. [1969] 2000. *The Psychology of the Child*. New York: Basic Books.

van Wijk, N. 2008. *Getting Started With Schemas: Revealing the Wonder-Full World of Children's Play*. New Lynn, Waitakere, Auckland: The New Zealand Playcentre Federation.

Deborah J. Leong and Elena Bodrova

Assessing and Scaffolding Make-Believe Play

It is the third week that Ms. Sotto's preschool classroom has been turned into an airport. The literacy center is a ticket counter, with a travel agency complete with child-made passports, tickets, and travel brochures. In the block area the children have constructed a walk-through X-ray scanner from cardboard boxes. A smaller box with openings on both ends functions as the screening device for carry-on luggage. There is an airplane cockpit made out of a big piece of cardboard with child-drawn instruments, an upside-down egg carton for a keyboard, and a paper plate that functions as the steering wheel.

Sophia tells her friend Vince that she is going on a trip and that she is going to forget to take out her water bottle. Then she won't be able to get through security. Vince says he is going to go to Puerto Rico where his grandmother lives. Sophia puts on her backpack and stands in line behind Vince. Finally it's her turn.

"Where are you going?" asks Tanya, the child behind the counter. "I'm goin' to Puerto Rico too." "OK. Here's your ticket to Puerto Rico. Your flight leaves at 77 o'clock." Tanya hands a piece of torn construction paper to Sophia. Sophia goes to another learning center and takes off her shoes. She puts them in a basket with her backpack, then pushes the basket through the scanner. Amir, who is the security guard, waits until Sophia walks through the X-ray frame, then waves a paper towel roll wand over her head. "OK," he says, "you can go now." Another security guard, Milda, is standing with Sophia's backpack, holding the bottle of water that Sophia "forgot" to take out of her backpack. "This is more than three ounces!" "Oh, I forgot. I'll put it in my cubby," says Sophia as she takes the bottle and runs to her cubby. Her next stop is the passenger lounge.

naeyc® 2, 3, 4

What is happening in Ms. Sotto's classroom is an example of what most early childhood educators mean when they talk about make-believe play—a fantasy world created by children where their imagination soars, their language expands, and their social skills multiply. Unfortunately, play observed in many early childhood classrooms rarely reaches this level; often children act out a series of simple and stereotypical scripts with little or no interaction with their peers. Research provides more and more evidence of the positive effects that well-developed play has on various areas of child development, such as children's social skills, emerging mathematical ability, mastery of early literacy concepts, and self-regulation (see Singer, Golinkoff, & Hirsh-Pasek 2006). It is also increasingly clear that without adult support, the play of many children is destined to never reach this fully developed status (Bodrova & Leong 2011). Teaching children to play has to be as intentional and systematic as teaching literacy or math and at the same time must take a form very different from adult-initiated practices often used to teach these content-related skills.

A Vygotskian Approach to Scaffolding Play

True to the saying that everything new is the "well-forgotten old," the answer to today's challenges comes from the past—from theories of play developed in the last century by Lev Vygotsky and his student Daniel Elkonin. These theories, along with the work done by students of Vygotsky and Elkonin, are the foundation of the approach to scaffolding play that we (the authors) currently use in our work with teachers in early childhood classrooms.

In Vygotsky ([1966] 1977) and Elkonin's (2005) view, make-believe play reaches its highest level of development in the preschool and kindergarten years. However, this fully developed or "mature" form of play does not emerge overnight. In fact, its earliest prerequisites develop in infancy, as babies learn to imitate other people's actions and begin to communicate by using gestures and vocalizations. Mastering language and forming emotional bonds with their caregivers prepare infants to learn from adults, who are their first "play mentors." It is important to make sure infants have ample opportunities to engage in playful interactions with adults during which they can practice their first pretend actions. In this sense a simple peekaboo game with an adult carries more educational value than any "smart toy" one gives to a child to play with alone.

Toddlers take further steps toward developing mature make-believe play as they move from mastering simple acts of putting on their clothes or brushing their hair to applying these acts to their dolls and stuffed animals; sometimes they even attempt to turn their pets into play partners. This is the time when adults' play mentoring and—even better—toddlers' participation in play with older children can change play from being "toy oriented" to "people oriented." As Elkonin (1978, 187) put it, "A child starts with feeding herself with a spoon; then she uses the spoon to feed everyone; then she uses the spoon to feed her doll; and finally feeds the doll pretending to be the 'mommy' who feeds her 'daughter'" (trans. by Bodrova). At this later stage, the play is no longer about the spoon and not even about a specific doll—it is about the relationship between mother and daughter.

Research provides more and more evidence of the positive effects that well-developed play has on children's social skills, emerging mathematical ability, mastery of early literacy concepts, and self-regulation.

Reaching preschool age does not guarantee, however, that a child's play stops being toy oriented. In fact, too many preschoolers continue to engage in play that would be appropriate for a 2-year-old but is something that 4-year-olds should have long outgrown. To help teachers support higher levels of play in these children, we have developed an approach to assessing and scaffolding play—PRoPELS—that focuses on its most critical elements (Bodrova & Leong 2007).

Minding One's Ps and Rs When Playing

PRoPELS is an acronym that stands for the most critical elements of children's play that can be assessed and scaffolded by adults.

Plan—children's ability to think about play in advance of playing

Roles children play—including the actions, language, and emotional expressions that are associated with a specific role

Props—the objects (real, symbolic, and imaginary) children use in play

Extended time frame—play that lasts for long stretches of time: within one play session for an hour or longer or extending over several play sessions and over several days

Language—what children say to develop a scenario or coordinate the actions of different players as well as speech associated with a particular role

Scenario—what children act out, including the sequence of scripts and interactions between roles

Using PRoPELS to assess play gives teachers an idea of how mature play is in their classrooms. On the continuum from most immature to most mature, children's make-believe play goes through five stages, with all of its elements (outlined above in the acronym PRoPELS) developing and expanding:

- The earliest stage—first scripts—is best described in terms of object-oriented pretend actions, such as a child playing with toy cars while making "vroom-vroom" sounds.
- An example of the next stage—roles in action—would be a child walking back and forth in high heels and, when asked, labeling her actions as playing "mommy."
- More mature play appears by stage 3—roles with rules and beginning scenarios. Children begin to coordinate their pretend actions with their play partners, making sure that these pretend actions go with the roles chosen by each of the players. When children are at this stage, it is common to hear them correcting each other's behaviors when the behaviors are not in line with the roles the children are playing.

Deborah J. Leong, PhD, is executive director of Tools of the Mind in Denver, Colorado. She is professor emerita of cognitive and developmental psychology at Metropolitan State University of Denver.

Elena Bodrova, PhD, is director of research and development at Tools of the Mind.

Deb and Elena coauthored *Tools of the Mind: The Vygotskian Approach to Early Childhood Education* and coauthored *Basics of Assessment: A Primer for Early Childhood Educators* (NAEYC) with Oralie McAfee.

For example, a child might comment if the patient starts playing with the doctor's stethoscope or the sales associate walks off wearing shoes she was about to sell to a customer.

- An example of stage 4 play—mature roles, planned scenarios, and symbolic props—is found in the opening vignette describing the airport play in Ms. Sotto's room. Children engage in multiple pretend actions, all being consistent with the roles they are playing while acting out complex scenarios.
- Finally, at stage 5—dramatization, multiple themes, multiple roles, and directors' play—planning and negotiating pretend actions starts to take more time than actually carrying them out. It is at this stage that children sometimes play multiple roles without actually having physical partners as they both "direct" and "act out" these roles with stuffed animals or even imaginary partners.

Five Stages in a Child's Make-Believe Play

	1. First Scripts	2. Roles in Action	3. Roles With Rules and Beginning Scenarios	4. Mature Roles, Planned Scenarios, and Symbolic Props	5. Dramatization, Multiple Themes, Multiple Roles, and Director's Play
Plan	Does not plan during play.	Does not plan during play.	Plans roles; actions are named prior to play.	Plans each scenario in advance.	Plans elaborate themes, scenarios, and complex roles. Spends more time planning than acting out the scenario.
Roles	Does not have roles.	Acts first and then decides on roles. No rules are revealed.	Has roles with rules that can be violated.	Has complex, multiple roles.	Can play more than one role at a time. Roles have social relationships.
Props	Plays with objects as objects.	Plays with objects as props. Actions with a prop result in a role.	Needs a prop for the role.	Chooses symbolic and pretend props.	Can pretend rather than actually have a prop. Does not need a prop to stay in the role. Objects can have roles.
Extended time frame	Explores objects, but not play scenarios.	Creates scenarios that last a few minutes.	Creates scenarios that last 10–15 minutes.	Creates scenarios that last 60 minutes or longer. With support, can create scenarios that last over several days.	Creates scenarios that last all day and over several days. Play can be interrupted and restarted.
Language	Uses little language.	Uses language to describe actions.	Uses language to describe roles and actions.	Uses language to describe roles and actions. Uses role speech.	Uses language to delineate the scenario, roles, and action. Book language is incorporated into role speech.
Scenario	Does not create a scenario. Can copy what the teacher does and says or will follow the teacher's directions if script is simple and repetitive.	Creates a scenario that is stereotypical, with limited behaviors. Can incorporate modeled roles and actions into play, with support.	Plays familiar scripts fully. Accepts new script ideas.	Plays a series of coordinated scenarios that change in response to previous ones or the desires of players. Describes unfolding scenario, roles, and actions.	Plays a series of coordinated scenarios that change in response to previous ones or the desires of players. Uses themes from stories and literature.

The table on page 29 summarizes the changes in the PRoPELS elements across different stages of play. Remember that the elements of play do not develop evenly within a stage. For example, a child may use props in play before developing role speech—language that fits the role—to use along with the props.

Many of the play skills that children learned in the past by observing and imitating their older playmates now have to be taught directly by teachers or learned from behaviors that teachers model.

What "PRoPELS" Play to New Heights?

The idea that we need to teach young children how to play is not a new one; until recently, however, it has been primarily discussed in terms of enhancing or facilitating play that has already reached a certain level of development. Explicit play instruction is often limited to the context of special education. While children with language delays or emotional disorders are thought to benefit from play interventions, children without such delays or disorders are usually expected to develop play skills on their own. This approach, while valid in the past, can no longer be adopted if we want all young children to develop mature play. Massive changes in the culture of childhood—such as the disappearance of multiage play groups, the increase in time children spend in adult-directed activities after school, and so on—mean that, for many young children, early childhood settings are the only place where they have the opportunity to learn how to play.

It is important to note, however, that learning how to play in the classroom will not look the same as learning to play within the informal neighborhood peer groups of yesterday. In the past, most play occurred in multiage groups in which younger children could learn from older "play experts," practice their play skills with peers of the same age, and then pass their knowledge on to other "play novices." Under those conditions, even preschoolers could act out elaborate and imaginative scenarios like castles or space travel, because the play skills of older children would buoy their own skills. In today's early childhood settings, children are almost always segregated by age and have to interact with play partners who are as inexperienced as they are. As a result, many of the play skills that children learned in the past by observing and imitating their older playmates now have to be taught directly by teachers or learned from behaviors that teachers model.

In addition, unlike the unstructured play of the past that often lasted for hours or days, playtime in today's early childhood classroom is limited and rarely exceeds one or two hours. This means that to achieve rapid progress in the quality of play, play scaffolding in the classroom needs to be designed to strategically target its most critical components: children's play **P**lanning, their ability to take on and maintain **R**oles, use of **P**rops, **E**xtended time frame, children's use of **L**anguage, and the quality of play **S**cenarios. In mature play, all of these discrete components are intertwined. However, we have found that at different levels of play, children will have more difficulty with one aspect or another. Use PRoPELS when you first observe children's play without intervening. After assessing the level of children's independent play, you can then decide what kind of scaffolding is the most appropriate. By highlighting the different areas in which you as the teacher can scaffold play, you can more efficiently support a given child or group of children.

Scaffolding children's play Planning. Elkonin (1978) identified planning as one of the features of mature play, describing the play of older children as consisting mostly of lengthy discussions of who is going to do what and how, followed by brief periods of acting out. As with other components of play, role and scenario planning can benefit from adult scaffolding. The teacher can start by asking children what they want to play or what they want to be, encouraging them to discuss the choice of the roles with their peers. Later, the teacher can ask children about more specific details of their future play scenarios, including what props they might need or whether they need to assume a different role. Children with special needs may need additional help in understanding their roles.

By making planning a necessary step in play, the teacher directs children's attention to the specifics of their roles and to the existence of rules associated with them. Many arguments that happen during play are over the fact that two children have chosen the same role or because the prop associated with that role is being used by another child. Planning prior to children going to a learning center can help prevent potential conflicts. Children can talk about the possible conflict instead of fighting over the prop. Planning allows children to discuss what might happen if there are two people who want to be truck drivers and only one truck. Having children agree to take turns before going to the center teaches social problem-solving strategies and starts the play off with positive interactions. Such discussions are particularly important for children with emotional or behavioral needs. Communicating clear expectations for behavior in a nonthreatening way will help prepare them for possible conflicts in play situations.

Families and Play

As you talk with families about the importance of play, use these points to discuss what children gain from their pretend play experiences and ways families can support children's learning through these experiences.

- Play is more than something that is fun, creative, and fosters children's imagination. It also **supports children's brain development** by helping them learn self-regulation—the capacity to control their impulses (both to stop doing something and to start doing something).
- We know from neuroscience research that **self-regulation benefits children**. In a classic experiment with marshmallows, children who delayed gratification longer at age 4 developed into adolescents who were more cognitively and socially competent, were more skilled at coping with frustration and stress, and had higher scholastic performance (Mischel, Shoda, & Rodriguez 1989). (To view part of a later version of this experiment, see www.youtube.com/watch?v=QX_oy9614HQ.)
- For pretend play to foster self-regulation, it **must include roles** (the child pretends to be someone else) with rules (when in character, the child can only do things that go with this role, not with other roles). For example, a child playing a baby can use a bottle but is not expected to eat with a fork. The pretend situation evolves as the play continues and the children react and interact together in their roles. A child goes to the "doctor" because he is sick, and the doctor listens to his heart and then gives the "patient" a prescription for some medicine. Play helps children practice delaying gratification because to stay in a role (e.g., a patient), the child needs to suppress his immediate desire (e.g., to play with the shiny stethoscope) and wait as the "doctor" examines him. Delaying gratification and planning future pretend scenarios with peers make role play an ideal venue for learning self-regulation.
- If children do not spend time with older siblings or children who model more sophisticated play skills, families can help them develop advanced play skills by **modeling how to pretend** and then having children imitate their actions. For example, with empty food boxes, play money, and a basket, a parent can model taking a trip to the grocery store.
- Using toys that are small replicas of real objects can help toddlers engage in pretend play, but such toys may limit the play of older children. These children can **use open-ended materials for props** or make their own. They might not even need to change the object—they just say what it is and what it does: "This block is going to be my cell phone and I'm going to pretend to call the pizza place and order a pizza."
- While running errands or doing chores, families can **point out the roles grownups play** so children can build those roles and situations into their play. "Did you notice that the cashier asked me if I had any coupons? I didn't, but when we play grocery store, we should cut out some coupons and use them. What did he ask me? 'Do you have . . .'"

Reference

Mischel, W., Y. Shoda, & M.I. Rodriguez. 1989. "Delay of Gratification in Children." *Science 244* (4907): 933–38.

The planning process can take place orally, but if children represent their plans in drawing or pretend writing, this process produces even greater benefits. First, as children engage in drawing, they are able to focus on their future play for a longer period of time, thus thinking over more details of their pretend scenarios. Second, having a tangible reminder helps children to regulate their own and their partners' behaviors; if a child has a picture of a veterinarian with her name on it, it becomes harder for another child to usurp this role. It also makes it easier for the teacher to troubleshoot possible conflicts and to engage children in brainstorming solutions. If two children want to be veterinarians, the teacher can introduce different kinds of veterinarians, such as the ones who take care of pets and those who treat large animals. Drawing a representation of their plans also enables children with expressive language needs to communicate their plans.

Planning also occurs during play when children change the scenario, the props, and the roles. Mature players discuss what is going to happen prior to it happening. For example, children might discuss what will happen at the fire station now that the fire is out. What other problems might happen? Children at the higher levels of play are able to plan on the fly, discuss possible directions for the scenarios, incorporate the ideas of the different players involved, and create props to match the changes in the play.

Scaffolding development and maintaining play Roles and rules. As Elkonin (1978) points out, the focus of mature play is the social roles and relationship between people—something that children cannot learn by simply observing adult behaviors. Therefore, to promote mature play, teachers need to explain the purpose of these behaviors, their sequence, the cause-and-effect relationships between different behaviors, and so on. For example, a teacher may explain that a customer in a restaurant cannot simply go to the kitchen and get a pizza—first he needs to give his order to a waiter. The waiter will take the order to a chef who will make the pizza, and only then will the customer be served the pizza. It also helps to discuss with the children what happens if the normal sequence of events gets disrupted; a chef who has not waited for the waiter to bring him a specific order may cook something different from what the customer wants to eat.

Having children agree to take turns before going to a learning center teaches social problem-solving strategies and starts the play off with positive interactions.

The rules that hold make-believe play together are not arbitrary but are based on the logic of real-life situations. Therefore, not knowing how these life scripts unfold will keep children from practicing self-regulated behaviors by following these rules. Helping children learn about scripts, and the rules that these scripts follow, calls for greater involvement by early childhood teachers in children's play than most teachers are used to. However, for most children this involvement needs to last for a relatively short time: soon they are able to use models provided by the teachers to build their own roles and rules, requiring only occasional adult support. More specific adult- or peer-supported planning may be necessary for dual language learners and for children with cognitive disabilities.

Scaffolding the use of Props in a symbolic way. Many young children today grow up using mostly realistic toys and having limited or no experience with using open-ended materials (e.g., a rock, stick, or paper plate) in play. This makes it difficult for them to develop a broad range of symbolic substitutions associated with higher levels of make-believe play. For these children, teachers need to model how to use props in a symbolic way, gradually expanding the repertoire of different uses for the same object. Over the period of several months, teachers can introduce more unstructured and multifunctional props while at the same time removing some overly realistic ones, such as plastic fried

eggs. Older preschoolers and kindergartners can start making their own props, while teachers can show younger preschoolers how to make minimal changes in the existing props to change their purpose. For example, a teacher can say, "Look at this big toy dog. We used it as the Big Bad Wolf when we played fairy tales. Do you think we can use it as the dalmatian in the fire station we are building now? What can we do to make this dog look like a dalmatian?"

Scaffolding the use of Language in play. An important part of adult scaffolding is monitoring children's language to make sure it is used in the service of play. For example, an adult's language should change to match the new ways props are used: the same paper plate that is a steering wheel in a fire truck today was a pretend pizza in the play restaurant last week. Since the appearance of the prop has not changed, the new name given to the paper plate is the only way the players will know that now it is being used in a new way. Assigning new names to the play props as these are used in new functions helps children master the symbolic nature of words, leading to children's eventual realization of the unique relationship that exists between words and the objects they signify. This emergence of metalinguistic awareness is associated with children's mastery of written language.

Language also touches some of the other elements of play described in PRoPELS. Adult scaffolding is needed to help children engage in "role speech," that is, using vocabulary, sentence structure, and intonation that fit a specific role. Teachers first introduce children to the ways people doing different jobs talk to each other during book reading or on a field trip. For example, children would learn that a 911 operator tries to reassure the person calling that the fire truck will arrive soon by saying, "Help is on the way." As the play unfolds, children may also need to be reminded of new vocabulary words they can use when playing a particular role. One way for the teacher to do this is to temporarily assume a secondary role, such as a customer or a patient, and make requests that prompt the children playing the leading roles of chefs, doctors, or vets to use these new words. For example, if the play in the pretend restaurant gets a little stale, a teacher can freshen it up by pretending to place a call to make a reservation. This would be a perfect opportunity to inquire about today's specials, the hours when the restaurant is open, whether kids' meals are available, and so on.

Mature players have scenarios that evolve and change as they play, hence the importance of providing extended periods of time for children to play.

Scaffolding development of play Scenarios that can unfold over Extended periods of time. A play scenario is what many people call the theme of play. It is the story line that the children are acting out. Children explore the social interactions of their roles through the play scenario. What happens when you go to the doctor's office? Your baby might be sick or you might have a broken leg. What will you say to the doctor? What will

Memo to: State Legislators
From: Vincent J. Costanza
Date: January 2015
Subject: Academic Rigor = Engaging Play

From an administrative perspective, why should you be the architect of programs that support bountiful and purposeful play? Here are a few of the reasons.

For one, children ought to have the same freedom to tinker, test, and experiment with ideas that any thoughtful adult experiences when the solution to a problem is novel and derived only by playing with a multitude of ideas. Imagine integrating the academic rigor required in the Common Core State Standards with the increasing demands of teacher evaluation systems without being afforded the opportunity to play with schedules, let alone ideas.

Speaking of academic rigor, this term cannot have any educational relevance to children unless combined with the notion of play. Administrators who are rightly concerned with offering rigorous experiences must ask, "What does academic rigor look like to a kindergarten child, for instance?" What rigor should look like to an administrator observing a kindergarten class is a classroom filled with children deeply engaged in meaningful activities and projects. Some children will be making mistakes, some children will be assisting peers, and all children will have the opportunity to play with ideas. In short, play is deep engagement.

By the way, I observe the same type of engagement described above when I see my local school district's high school robotics team fiddling, messing around, working with peers, and occasionally speaking with adults. Despite the noise and boxes of pizza that often accompany the workings of the robotics team, would anyone dare claim that the play they engage in is not academically rigorous? Rather than wonder why more children do not engage in play experiences like those of the robotics team, maybe we should design programs that incorporate such play throughout a child's schooling.

Take a moment to play with that idea for a little.

Vincent J. Costanza, EdD, is the executive director of the Race to the Top–Early Learning Challenge (RTT-ELC) with the New Jersey Department of Education, Division of Early Childhood Education.

he or she do to help you? Mature players have scenarios that evolve and change as they play, hence the importance of providing extended periods of time for children to play.

Scaffolding play scenarios has several components. First, children often lack background knowledge to build their scenarios. Even to play "family dinner" or "grocery store," which many children are expected to be familiar with, requires knowledge of the setting, roles, and actions associated with these scenarios. To build background knowledge about less familiar topics, teachers use field trips, visiting experts, and books and videos. To promote mature play, the choice of places to take children on a field trip and the choice of books and videos need to be guided by how well these activities and tools will help children to learn about people and their activities.

When field trips or books center on objects or animals, such as a trip to the zoo or a book on dinosaurs, very little of their content gets reenacted in mature make-believe play. However, if a teacher supplements a book on dinosaurs with additional videos and books portraying the work of paleontologists, children are more likely to start playing pretend scenarios, such as museum or dinosaur dig, and incorporate new concepts in their conversations.

Sometimes even a very successful field trip may not provide enough information for children to transfer what they saw on this trip to their play in the classroom. In these cases teachers have to support play by modeling pretend actions and role speech more explicitly, for example, role-playing and practicing some of the pretend actions with children. For most children such intensive "play practice" is needed for only a limited time. Other children, such as children with special needs, can benefit from more extensive play practice with their peers.

Conclusion

Mature make-believe play is an important and unique context, providing opportunities to learn not afforded by other classroom activities. It should not be considered something extra that can be cut to accommodate more time for academic skills, nor should it be used as a means of adding "entertainment value" for inherently boring and decontextualized drills. Instead, play should be preserved and nurtured as one of the "uniquely 'preschool'" (in the words of Vygotsky's colleague and student Alexander Zaporozhets) activities that provide the most beneficial context for children's development:

> Optimal educational opportunities for a young child to reach his or her potential and to develop in a harmonious fashion are not created by accelerated ultra-early instruction aimed at shortening the childhood period—that would prematurely turn a toddler into a preschooler and a preschooler into a first-grader. What is needed is just the opposite—expansion and enrichment of the content in the activities that are uniquely "preschool": from play to painting to interactions with peers and adults. (Zaporozhets 1986, 88)

References

Bodrova, E., & D.J. Leong. 2007. *Tools of the Mind: The Vygotskian Approach to Early Childhood Education.* 2nd ed. Upper Saddle River, NJ: Pearson Education.

Bodrova, E., & D. Leong. 2011. "Revisiting Vygotskian Perspectives on Play and Pedagogy." Chap. 5 in *Rethinking Play and Pedagogy in Early Childhood Education: Concepts, Contexts and Cultures*, ed. S. Rogers, 60–72. New York: Routledge.

Elkonin, D.B. 1978. *Psychologija igry* [The Psychology of Play]. Moscow: Pedagogika.

Elkonin, D.B. 2005. "Chapter 1: The Subject of Our Research: The Developed Form of Play." *Journal of Russian and East European Psychology* 43 (1): 22–48.

Singer, D.G., R.M. Golinkoff, & K. Hirsh-Pasek, eds. 2006. *Play = Learning: How Play Motivates and Enhances Children's Cognitive and Social-Emotional Growth*. New York: Oxford University Press.

Vygotsky, L.S. [1966] 1977. "Play and Its Role in the Mental Development of the Child." In *Soviet Developmental Psychology: An Anthology*, ed. M. Cole, 76–99. White Plains, NY: M.E. Sharpe.

Zaporozhets, A.V. 1986. *Izbrannye psychologicheskie trudy* [Selected Works in Psychology]. Moscow: Pedagogika.

Genan T. Anderson, Anita Rae Spainhower, and Ann C. Sharp

"Where Do the Bears Go?" The Value of Child-Directed Play

"Where do the bears go?" 4-year-old Tyler asks.

"Not with the lions. They'll fight," replies Juan, a 5-year-old.

By adding a basket of stuffed bears to the classroom zoo, Ms. Ellison, a preschool teacher, intentionally creates disequilibrium in the children's play. The bears are new to their zoo and now need a place to be. Keeping the bears inside the basket just doesn't work for either Tyler or Juan, but putting them in the same space as the lions isn't a choice Juan is willing to consider. Ms. Ellison uses a change in the environment to create an opportunity for these children to work together to solve a problem they find important. Because solving any problem requires creative and critical thinking, the skills these children learn in solving the problem of the bear enclosure will be useful to them as they tackle other problems. Playing and working together, they will look at ideas in different ways and construct new knowledge (Riley & Jones 2010).

Child-Directed Play Induces Problem Solving

"We'll have to build another cereal box house," Juan says.

"NO!" Tyler is quick to respond. "Don't you remember, this one took a hundred days?"

"No, it didn't," Juan says, defiantly. "Ms. Ellison, Tyler says it took a hundred days to build our cereal box house."

When children are responsible for solving a problem together, different

naeyc® 2, 3

ideas, perspectives, and opinions may result in conflict. The children place lions in a house they built together from empty cereal boxes. The size of the basket of bears makes Juan think they will need a space as large as the one they gave to the lions, so building a new cereal box house seems to be the ideal solution to their problem. Tyler, on the other hand, remembers how long it took them to collect boxes and construct the original cereal box house as "a hundred days," or a very, very long time. For Tyler, the solution Juan proposes is impossible. At an impasse, Juan turns to the teacher for help.

"Hmmmm," replies Ms. Ellison. "Let's go look on the calendar for the day we began, and you can count."

The boys hurry to the home center where their classroom calendar hangs. They quickly flip back the pages and begin counting from April 10. It takes several tries before the boys agree that they built the house in just 43 days.

Instead of telling the children the information they need, Ms. Ellison provides scaffolding to help the boys access previous knowledge and use their math skills to solve the problem. This teaching strategy serves two purposes: the children have a meaningful way to practice previously learned skills, and they resolve a conflict regarding information the boys remembered differently.

Child-Directed Play Enriches Math Learning

Ms. Ellison taught calendar concepts in the context of the sociodramatic play. Because time is very abstract and especially difficult for preoperational thinkers (ages 2–7) to understand (Piaget 1977), a calendar hangs in the home center to help children better understand this concept. Dates are circled and labeled for important classroom events. The children often decide whether a date should be circled and if they need to count how many days it is until the event will occur. They had marked the first day of construction for their cereal box house and the day they finished it.

Even though Ms. Ellison is nearby to support them in their counting, she leaves the responsibility of arriving at an accurate count to the children. They apply the concepts of consecutive counting, one-to-one correspondence, and an understanding of the days of the week. Because their project spanned more than one calendar month, they apply concepts of day, week, and month to answer their question. The play has led to practice of previously learned skills in an authentic and meaningful context.

Four-year-old Megan immediately reports that with only eight school days left, they cannot make a bear's house in time. "In eight days, it is summer," she says. "It's marked right here on the 24. I circled it last week."

A heated yet constructive discussion begins among several children as they try to decide whether it is possible to build another cereal box house.

Estimation and concept of number are very apparent in Megan's understanding of time. With the new information—there are only eight days until school is out for the summer—it is clear to Megan that Juan's idea to build another cereal box house will not work. Not all of her classmates come to the same conclusion. At this stage of development, they are teetering between the perspectives of "What I am thinking, you are thinking, too" and "There may be two perspectives, and yours may be different from mine" (Piaget 1977). Ms. Ellison allows the debate to continue until it is apparent that the children cannot examine a viewpoint or idea that is not their own.

Genan T. Anderson, PhD, is the early childhood program coordinator and professor of elementary education at Utah Valley University (UVU), in Orem. Genan champions play in early childhood programs through teaching, professional writing, and presentations.

Anita Rae Spainhower is head teacher of UVU Laboratory Preschool and an adjunct professor. Anita has been an early childhood educator for more than 35 years, working in private and corporate child care, Head Start, and university settings.

Ann C. Sharp, PhD, is an assistant professor at UVU, where she teaches literacy methods to preservice teachers. Ann is interested in preserving playfulness in literacy instruction while simultaneously applying research-based methods.

The discussion is interrupted by Ms. Ellison's quiet comment, "I wonder what Hyun is building in the block center?"

Juan and Tyler are the first to reach Hyun and ask her what she is building with the large wooden blocks and planks. Before she can answer, they are already asking if the bears could live there.

"That's what it is," Hyun answers. "It's a bear cave. It's the Big Hungry Bear's cave."

Scaffolding serves two purposes: the children have a meaningful way to practice previously learned skills, and they resolve a conflict regarding information the boys remembered differently.

Child-Directed Play Requires Symbol Representation

Hyun bypasses the group attempt to find a home for the bears and goes directly to the block center to build a bear cave. The fact that in her mind it is the Big Hungry Bear's cave reflects her recall of a favorite story that the teacher has read aloud and made available in the library corner. Hyun remembers that bears live in caves. Using concepts of symmetry, shape, and size, she builds a structure large enough to comfortably house the full basket of bears and still have room for the zookeeper to enter to feed and care for them.

Through her play, Hyun has learned the concept that one thing can be two things at the same time, or that she can use one thing to represent another thing (Elkind 2007). She uses basic blocks to represent a cave, just as the cereal boxes represent a lion's den. This representation concept will serve her well as she learns that letters are used to represent sounds and are combined to make words that represent things and ideas. One word can have two meanings. One set of letters can be two different words. Numerals represent a specific number of objects, and symbols represent mathematical operations.

Child-Directed Play Enriches Literacy

Not entirely satisfied, Megan states clearly that there is no way to tell which is the lion house and which is the bear cave. The children seem stumped.

After a moment or two, Ms. Ellison, who is keenly aware of Megan's interest in writing, casually comments, "I wonder if signs would help?"

Megan excitedly hurries to the writing center and begins creating signs. Soon she is joined by three friends who help complete the signs. With tape and signs in hand, the children begin labeling.

The writing center borders the home center so that the children have easy access to the materials they need to incorporate written and oral language into their play. In the first week of school, children learn about the use, purpose, and care of the wide variety of supplies and tools in the writing center. All items are immediately available for their use.

Creating a literacy-enriched play environment reflects the belief that literacy is found in every part of our lives. Although taught intentionally during a specific time of the day, writing instruction is purposefully embedded throughout the day.

Children practice their literacy skills because those tools are essential to their play. So it naturally follows that literacy becomes intricately woven into the children's play (Lillard et al. 2013). They use play to direct their learning, gaining understanding through self-created learning experiences (Elkind 2007).

Megan's signs are accurately spelled and accompanied by illustrations. The other signs are accurate sound spellings—for example, BERZ KAV. Shamia determines that initials will do; her sign reads A R H B T K S. When asked for interpretation, she reports, "It says, 'Alligators are here because they can swim.'"

Early Learning Standards Addressed in This Play Scenario

Emotional

- Learn the skills needed to regulate their emotions, behavior, and attention
- Develop a sense of competence and positive attitudes toward learning, such as persistence, engagement, curiosity, and mastery

Social Studies

- Become a part of the classroom community; feel accepted and have a sense of belonging
- Develop skills for entering into social groups, developing friendships, helping, and other prosocial behaviors
- Explore social roles in the family and workplace through play and learn about the community
- Build a foundation for understanding economic concepts (e.g., by playing restaurant, managing a store, and identifying and exchanging money)

Oral Language and Conflict Resolution

- Interact positively, respectfully, and cooperatively with others; learn from and with one another; and resolve conflicts in constructive ways
- Learn to understand, empathize with, and take into account other people's perspectives
- Use and understand oral and written communication
- Develop competence in verbal and nonverbal communication by responding to questions; communicating needs, thoughts, and experiences; and describing things and events
- Develop vocabulary through conversations, experiences, and books

Writing

- Become familiar with print through active involvement in making sense of print, and by having opportunities to become familiar with, recognize, and use print that is accessible throughout the classroom
- Write (including scribbling, making letter-like marks, and using developmental spelling) using writing materials and activities readily available in multiple centers
- Write on their own, through access to the alphabet and to printed words about topics of interest

Mathematics

- Build an understanding of numbers, number names, and their relationships to object qualities and to symbols
- Build an understanding of time in the context of their lives, schedules, and routines
- Integrate mathematical terms into everyday conversation
- Understand the concept of measurement by using standard and nonstandard units of measurement

Science

- Categorize by one or two attributes such as shape, size, and color
- Learn key content and principles of science

Creative Arts

- Express ideas and feelings creatively

Adapted from NAEYC (2014), 8–24. © NAEYC.

While Megan is capable of sound spelling, she usually prefers the "real way." The words on Megan's signs are spelled correctly because she either asked a teacher to spell them or copied labels in the writing center. Shamia has picked up on the teacher's earlier instruction that there are many times people don't want to take the time or use up the space to write their entire name, so they use initials. The other children use their knowledge of letter sounds to represent the words they are writing. Through their play, the children practice and stretch their language skills, build vocabulary, and experiment and figure out how language works.

When all the signs are appropriately hung, the children announce, "We are the sign makers for the zoo!"

Through their play, the children practice and stretch their language skills, build vocabulary, and experiment and figure out how language works.

Child-Directed Play Is Carefully Scaffolded

In response to this announcement, Ms. Ellison uses the gathering time that follows center time to lead the children in a webbing activity titled Jobs at the Zoo.

As the children name the zoo workers, Ms. Ellison writes the job titles inside ovals on a whiteboard around the central oval titled Jobs at the Zoo. Writing the job titles provides a visual representation of the roles children may assume during their play and also models how letters form words that represent ideas.

During the webbing activity, a lively discussion occurs around feeding the animals—what they prefer to eat and how they get their food.

"The lions just leave and go get some meat and then come back," says 4-year-old Brian. "No one can stop them."

"No, they don't," 5-year-old Jaelee responds quickly. She is a regular zoo patron. "People feed them. They feed them at the same time every day. I saw them!"

In the context of their play, the children's ideas on how the animals get their food become explicit. In Brian's *schema*—the mental framework he uses to organize new information—the lions leave their enclosures to obtain food, but Jaelee's experience challenges Brian's existing ideas. After listening to the discussion and noting the many inaccuracies being suggested and accepted by the group, Ms. Ellison adds new information by showing a video on zoo dieticians and animal diets. The discussion that follows forces Brian to look at his schema of lions getting meat from an entirely different perspective. The social interactions in the play press Brian to accommodate the new information by creating a new understanding of how zoo lions obtain meat.

Families and Play

Families with young children have many responsibilities. These include providing and joining in daily experiences that encourage children to imagine, discover, explore, and understand the world. One way for families to promote these experiences is through constructive play with three-dimensional objects.

One mother did this by creating a Concoction Box for her young children. She filled the box with open-ended, curiosity-arousing objects that begged to be touched, including red and blue foam pieces, wooden blocks, shiny gold and silver domes, wooden dowels, white foam wedges, and remnants of picture frames. At first the children turned the objects over and over, their brains carefully noting the physical properties—what shape and color the materials were; their smell and texture; and how strong, tough, elastic, dense, and flexible they were. Then they began to imagine and wonder what they could do with these items. Could they stack them on top of each other? Lay them side by side? Could they make a pattern based on colors, shapes, or other attributes of the objects? Could they use them to represent something important, like the farm they had visited the week before or that tall building in the city where Grandma worked? Could they create something that no one had ever seen before?

Over time, as they tried out all these possibilities and more, the children generated knowledge, developed their thinking abilities, and gained a sense of confidence. These are skills that will shape who they become as adults, giving them the tools to succeed at home, in their workplaces, and in their social lives. Children who apply initiative and take reasonable risks become adults who seize opportunities while also making careful calculations about the risks. These personal qualities are highly prized by employers. Children who can focus, imagine, make connections, pay close attention to detail, problem solve, create, and innovate become adults who are successful leaders, engineers, accountants, artists, bankers, or writers. What children experience in the early years supports learning and achievement now and in the future.

—**Marcia L. Nell,** PhD, Millersville University, and **Walter F. Drew,** EdD, Institute for Self Active Education

Child-Directed Play Provides Opportunities for Decision Making

At center time the following day, the children are highly motivated to create a zoo kitchen. The home center is the logical location. Bowls, measuring cups, and plastic fruits and vegetables are already present. The children ask Ms. Ellison to fill the sensory table with sand and place it in the home center so they can include the sand in their zoo recipes.

"But we need water," 5-year-old Austin claims. Fully aware that water has never been allowed in the home center, he glances at Ms. Ellison to see her reaction to his request. When there is no verbal response, he begins his defense.

"The cook in the video used water for everything. It makes the food soft, and it cleans up the messes. I only need a little, or maybe a lot." He pauses. With only a smile from the teacher, he knows his idea has been approved.

Immediately, he begins recruiting friends to make the long trip across the room from the sink to the zoo kitchen with measuring cups of water in hand. "I need five cups for the monkey mush," he instructs. He counts off five friends.

"Walk slow and careful if your cup is full. Or you can fill it halfway and go twice." Pausing to think, he then says, "Yes, if it's half full you have to go twice."

Four-year-old Qamar, listening well but always able to come up with ideas of her own, says, "Not me. I'm going to carry two cups and go one time."

Austin has internalized the rule of no water in the home center, but it doesn't work with his play. He is clearly confident enough to share this disequilibrium with the teacher, pressing his point until he receives the desired concession. Still, he respects the reason for the rule. The water is far away from the home center, and it may spill when it is carried from the sink to his table. Trying to stay within this boundary, he verbalizes his defense for an exception by explaining different solutions. These important decisions that emerge in the narrative of the children's play help them see cause and effect and aid in their self-regulation (Riley & Jones 2010).

Austin organizes the crew by using one-to-one correspondence to select five friends to retrieve five cups of water. That works if they each carry a full cup, but if they carry only half a cup to avoid spilling, then there won't be enough water. He demonstrates an automatic response to the relationship of half to whole when he instructs the children to then go to the sink for water twice. Qamar carries that concept one step further when she announces that she can carry two half-full cups at the same time and arrive with one full cup in one trip. When the children do math with their bodies in the context of their unfolding story, motivation and long-term retention are greatly enhanced. In fact, Riley and Jones (2010) claim that learning beyond facts requires active involvement.

During another structured group time, the children transform a large cardboard box into a zoo train, then paint and decorate it with animals. Each day, the children add blocks for chairs. There is room for six passengers and a conductor. Snacks are available for passengers, and children make tickets in the writing center.

These children are confident decision makers. With an idea of the elements of the zoo train, they rearrange the materials in the classroom to meet the staging requirements of their story. Positive feelings of self-efficacy are evident in the control the children exhibit over the materials in their environment and over their own actions. The many choices teachers offer help these children make wise decisions and be comfortable with their outcomes (Riley & Jones 2010).

Child-Directed Play Aids Development of Self-Regulation

Jaelee takes over the ticket-writing process and instructs the others to write down what it costs to ride the train. Most children write numbers from 1 to 9, but indicate that it means nine dollars. A few ask how to make their tickets say $1.00, so Ms. Ellison writes a model on the whiteboard in the writing center.

Jaelee illustrates a sign and asks the teacher to write "Buy Tickets Here" on it. She hangs it on the cabinet near the train, and puts the tickets in an oatmeal box from the home center.

She stands by faithfully, making sure everyone purchases a ticket before entering the train box.

"How many would you like?" she asks, in a really sappy, sweet voice. "Enjoy your ride."

The pitch and tone of Jaelee's voice reflect her understanding of the character she portrays in their story—matching, no doubt, the voice of the ticket taker at her local zoo. While every child who visits the zoo asks for a ride on the train, the rules about tickets and money, snacks, and even "enjoying the ride," become more clear as they incorporate these elements into their play.

Jaelee delegates the ticket sales to 4-year-old Peter after 11 minutes and returns to the writing center to make more tickets. She is close enough to Peter to correct his ticket-selling approach quite often!

Jaelee understands the rule about purchasing a ticket before riding the train at the zoo and is very precise in regulating her peers' observance of that rule. She knows her role in the play and stays in character without trying to assume the role of conductor or passenger played by other classmates. She maintains that role for an extended period

Memo to: Funders of Early Childhood Programs
From: Sandra Waite-Stupiansky
Date: January 2015
Subject: Why Play Is Learning at Its Best

Play is the most important way that young children learn. Through play, children learn about the social, physical, emotional, and cognitive worlds around them. As they play with adults, they learn new vocabulary, understand culturally determined rules and roles such as how to treat one another, and build important emotional connections. When they play with their peers, they learn that others have perspectives, rights, and feelings that may conflict with their own. Playing with others is how children learn reciprocity and mutual respect, essential traits humans need to coexist in a peaceful world.

Play is the way that children learn resilience and perseverance. When obstacles come their way, young children find playful ways to overcome small barriers with persistence, gumption, and skill. When they fall, they get back up. If their creations don't work out the first time, they try and try again. These lessons stick with them for life.

Play is the way that children stretch themselves. They challenge themselves to jump higher, build taller, and concentrate longer. They try out new words and make them their own. Children don't need rewards for playing. Play is satisfying in its own right.

Play is the way children learn what it is like to be an adult as they try on adult roles. They feed the baby and put him to bed, or build the next rocket ship to the moon. Anything is possible in play.

Play is the way that children learn to deal with tension and stress. They pretend to be monsters and superheroes in the battle of good versus evil—and of course good always wins.

So why should play be funded? It is learning at its best—authentic, natural, and intrinsically rewarding. What could be better?

Sandra Waite-Stupiansky, PhD, is a professor of early childhood and reading at Edinboro University, in Pennsylvania.

before finding another job her character needs to do, and then delegates the actual ticket sales to Peter.

Even though Jaelee allows Peter to sell the tickets while she makes more, she continues to monitor his performance and coaches and corrects him as she feels necessary. Peter is willing to accept Jaelee's directions regulating his behavior so he can remain part of the zoo train play. The train scenario within the zoo narrative represents very high levels of skill in social interaction. Not only are these children regulating one another, they are accepting regulation from one another and self-regulating. The self-regulation learned in sociodramatic play will be transferred to other activities and increase their performance in all learning domains (Bodrova & Leong 2007).

Conclusion

The children's delighted excitement, serious decisions, and focus on creating cohesiveness in the story as it unfolds could be value enough for defending the importance of child-directed, sociodramatic play—and yet the learning that happens in the play is so much more. The conflict inherent in sociodramatic play gives children opportunities to practice thinking critically to solve the problems that emerge. Decision making during play leads to children's positive self-efficacy and confidence in their control over themselves and their environment. When the play becomes more important than individual egos and ideas, children begin to regulate others and to self-regulate. As play stories unfold, they offer many chances for children to apply fundamental literacy and math skills for authentic purposes. Perhaps most important, child-directed play is a joyful part of childhood that early childhood professionals should guard and preserve for the children they teach.

References

Bodrova, E., & D.J. Leong. 2007. *Tools of the Mind: The Vygotskian Approach to Early Childhood Education.* 2nd ed. Upper Saddle River, NJ: Pearson Education.

Elkind, D. 2007. *The Power of Play: Learning What Comes Naturally.* Philadelphia: Da Capo.

Lillard, A.S., M.D. Lerner, E.J. Hopkins, R.A. Dore, E.D. Smith, & C.M. Palmquist. 2013. "The Impact of Pretend Play on Children's Development: A Review of the Evidence." *Psychological Bulletin* 139 (1): 1–34.

NAEYC. 2014. *NAEYC Early Childhood Program Standards and Accreditation Criteria and Guidance for Assessment.* www.naeyc.org/files/academy/file/AllCriteriaDocument.pdf.

Piaget, J. 1977. *The Essential Piaget: An Interpretive Reference and Guide.* Ed. and trans. H.E. Gruber & J.J. Vonèche. New York: Basic Books.

Riley, J.G., & R.B. Jones. 2010. "Acknowledging Learning Through Play in the Primary Grades." *Childhood Education* 86 (3): 146–9.

Timothy A. Kinard

Flying Over the School: Superhero Play—Friend or Foe?

You may think a child is listening to a math lesson, but he is Superman in a cape flying over the top of the school.
—Vivian Gussin Paley, NAEYC Radio

For decades Vivian Paley (1988, 2004) has shared her stories of children's fantasy play. She skillfully weaves words into images, painting a picture of the tension between children's desires for superhero-themed play and adults' values about this kind of play. This article explores the way these themes and desires are addressed at one early childhood setting.

Enter a preschool playground in Central Texas. The temperature is over 100°F, but most of the day is spent outside. Many children are barefoot, shirtless. Teachers and children interact in every shaded spot. They pile sand. Tell stories. Ride trikes and bikes. Wooden playhouses are temporary homes to pretend families, rescuers, soldiers, royalty—and to superheroes.

I have come here as a researcher, observing the interactions between the children and their teachers. As teachers go through their daily routines, I follow them around. I ask them questions during the times when they are not teaching, as when they rake the sandy playground before the beginning of the school day, scouring the landscape for hidden dangers. I tag along as they set up inviting displays of colorful liquids and powders, or chunks of clay.

At this moment, a teacher named Leandra has drawn a small crowd of 3-, 4-, and 5-year-olds, creating a gleeful mosh pit with herself in the middle. It is a vibrant, spontaneous circle time, teeming with excited talk. She leans forward, brush in hand, painting with care. Her canvas is Carlos's bare back. She painstakingly renders the Superman logo in the middle of a flowing red cape she has emblazoned across his shoulders.

The other girls and boys in the circle await their turns to get painted. But they do not wait passively. They use the time to contribute to decision making about the designs that will adorn their bodies and the characters, plots, and play that will follow. Many ask to be turned into superheroes. Some want only an emblem painted on a cheek. Some go for the full-body treatment—insignias on their chests, boots painted down their shins, capes on their backs, masks across their faces, even belts and armbands. Carlos bursts from the circle and dashes across the playground, joining the play of painted peers.

Body painting has evolved into a ritual at this school. Trays of washable, nontoxic watercolor paints are playground staples. Children and teachers treat them as mobile dress-up boxes. Although every imaginable character has emerged from the paint trays, superheroes are recurring themes. Superman, Batman, and Wonder Woman are favorites, but children often create invented, personalized superheroes. Custom color schemes, logos, and superpowers are integral parts of the children's decision-making process.

This is a celebration of individuality *and* commonality, a shared interest between children and teachers that creates a space in the curriculum for sustained sociodramatic play and a forum for dialogue about superheroes' actions. These teachers understand what Paley has articulated—children have a passion for superhero play.

Planning is critical for supporting mature play that is rife with academic and social benefits, like concentration and determination, and opportunities to practice taking other points of view.

Rowdiness and Violence: Are Superheroes a Problem?

Young children love playing superhero, but this kind of play is usually rambunctious and nearly always has violent content. Superheroes are vigilantes, maverick fighters who seem not to follow rules. It is worth wondering whether the rowdiness associated with superhero play makes it hard for children to calm down and do more focused explorations afterward. It is also worth wondering whether playing superhero leads to accepting that fighting for right means fighting *is* right.

Becoming Batman

Eli is 4 years old when I first meet him at this school. He is a Batman fan. Each morning he strips off his shirt and asks to be painted as Batman. Eli, Leandra, and the children who gather around engage in a dialogue about what he will do as Batman—who will play with him and what tools he needs to accomplish his goals. Leandra, Eli, and Eli's peers *plan*, with the children practicing their "ability to think about play in advance of playing" (Leong & Bodrova 2015, 28). Planning is one of the most critical elements for supporting higher levels of play (Leong & Bodrova 2015), the type of mature play that is rife with academic and social benefits, like concentration and determination, and opportunities to practice taking other points of view.

As soon as he is painted, Eli's demeanor morphs into his understanding of Batman. His typically jovial face takes on a stern look, and his bouncy gait becomes purposeful and regulated. Then Batman begins interacting with Superman, played by 4-year-old Felix. The two bolt about the playground, punching and kicking the air, grappling with invisible foes. They do not break character, and they use the dialogue of the two superheroes

Timothy A. Kinard, PhD, is an assistant professor of curriculum and instruction at Texas State University–San Marcos. A former preschool and kindergarten teacher, Tim currently researches taken-for-granted notions in early childhood education and co-runs a program where preservice teachers and 3- to 7-year-olds make discoveries together through play and storytelling.

Mature play has clearly defined rules and roles. As children follow the rules in play, they learn to delay immediate fulfillment of their desires.

to further the plot and actions of their play (Lillard et al. 2013). "Superman! Look over there! It's bad ninjas! Use your laser eyes!" The narrative they establish fosters language arts skills, like development of a plot and a resolution, as well as interpersonal skills like negotiation (Cooper 2009; Quintero 2009).

> Both superheroes stand atop a pyramid of recycled rubber tires. Superman suddenly jumps from the pyramid and flies away, his arms stretched out before him. Eli resituates his feet in preparation for flying after his super-friend. But before he can leap, Superman calls out behind him, "Batman, you can't fly, so just wait there! I'll bring the crystals for the ship!"
>
> For a moment, a very *un*-Batman-looking expression takes shape beneath Eli's painted blue mask: disappointment. But the look suddenly changes, and one of resolve takes its place. Eli knows his favorite superhero is written as a character unable to fly. This is an understood rule of the negotiated play the boys share. Batman's steely look returns, and he calls out, "OK, Superman! I'll wait here!" After a few long minutes, the two are reunited and resume putting crystals in their imagined spaceship.

Analyzing Eli's Superpowers

I can scarcely imagine a better example of a child behaving "as though he were a head taller than himself" than Eli becoming Batman (Vygotsky 1978, 102). He imagines himself well beyond his own limited abilities. "Play seems to be invented at the point when the child begins to experience unrealizable tendencies" (93), and Eli meets this challenge in "an imaginary, illusory world in which unrealizable desires can be realized" (93).

But these rambunctious fantasy characters are not vehicles for learning rowdiness. In Eli's imagined world a strict set of rules is in place. When he leaves the painting circle with a yellow oval on his chest—and the familiar bat silhouette within it—he walks into a highly structured world where his behaviors are tightly controlled by his understandings of the Batman character. He has to act the part. Bodrova, Germeroth, and Leong (2013) define "mature play" as the kind of play that follows clearly defined rules and roles and utilizes the delay of instant gratification in order to maintain those rules and roles—essential skills in negotiating a socially complex world.

Acquiring Self-Regulatory Skills

"When a boy acts out the role of a daddy making breakfast, he is limited by all the rules of daddy-ness" (Tough 2009, 32). In restricting himself to the rules he establishes for the character of Batman, Eli has to limit his desire to fly so he can stay in the story line that he and Felix have negotiated for themselves. "Stimulating experiences where children can practice behavioral self-regulation in child-centered activities are important" in the development of executive function (McClelland et al. 2007, 99). *Executive function* is the ability to set goals, be cognitively flexible, process information, and maintain concentration (Anderson & Reidy 2012). Executive function is essential to the skill of self-regulation (Obradović, Portilla, & Boyce 2012). And "self-regulatory skills are critical for [children] to become engaged in the early academic opportunities, social relationships, and contexts that support their future development" (Rimm-Kaufman & Wanless 2012, 301). Eli exercises this function in setting aside his own desires in favor of being Batman. He does what is expected of him within the play scenario.

At Eli's school, when Leandra is painting children, she creates an opportunity for the soon-to-be superheroes to manage themselves by engaging in a ritual that is both voluntary and highly desired by the children. They share the space with skill, weighing the consequences of pushing away someone who comes into their personal space with a desire to peacefully share the social space. Examples of this abound at this school: children learn self-regulation by negotiating with peers ways to engage in activities of their own choosing. What looks rambunctious actually creates self-discipline.

Does Violence-Tinged Play Glorify Violence?

Practicing self-regulation through rambunctious play is an answer to only one of the vexing questions superhero play brings up. What about the violence? Does pretending to fight create fighters? Does playing violent games teach that violence is tolerated? Urban, the school's director, describes his thoughts on violence-tinged play in terms of the benefits of sociodramatic play in general and as a way to invite dialogue *about* violence:

> Play is key. Their ideas. Their stories. But we could say, "No, no, no. We can't play fighting games, because hitting is wrong. Fighting is bad." We *do* think fighting is bad. We *do* think hitting is wrong, but we want to *invite* Batman play into our school, so we can have a conversation about it.

Urban is comfortable with observers seeing children acting out violent scenarios at the school. He believes actions that look controversial in the moment can provide opportunities for the children to develop sophisticated social understandings. Superheroes are symbols of power, but when children pretend to be powerful, it does not necessarily mean they will someday abuse power. In fact, they might learn to better manage power by playing out scenarios involving it (Kinard 2014).

Families and Play

I am the father of three daughters, and like all parents, I have questions and concerns about my children's healthy development. Two of my biggest questions are how to help my children learn to be kind and how to teach them not only to read but also to *love* reading. Below are my thoughts as an educator about ways early childhood settings—and specifically play—support children's development in these areas.

How Play Helps Children Learn to Be Kind

To learn kindness children must learn that others have emotions just like their own. This is a social process, and it happens beautifully through playing with others. There is a difference between being in a peer group and playing with peers. Simply *being* together (such as at group time) might not be enough. When children *play* with peers at a young age, they learn through powerful experience the language of others' emotional states. Therefore, it is vital that young children play together in settings where play is valued and peers are ample. Early childhood programs are the perfect settings for this. As children shift from playing *next to* others to playing *with* them, they learn to read each other's needs through the narratives—or story lines—of their play. As children learn what their peers need, they also learn to value those needs. This is a gateway to learning kindness.

How Play Narratives Help Children Learn to Read and Develop a Love of Reading

It takes abstract and symbolic thinking to understand that letters are symbols that represent sounds and that, strung together, they blend to represent meaningful combinations of sound. When young children create play scenarios in which an object is used to represent something else—like a wooden block for a cell phone—they are practicing representing something that is not really there. This is a vital step toward the kind of thinking that allows symbols on a page to stand for a string of sounds.

However, there is much more to reading than knowing letters and deciphering words. To understand that authors convey messages through written words, children must learn to understand that there is such a thing as "narrative." Books have narratives—a story or theme presented across time that unfolds informatively or engagingly for the reader. Reading to children gives them experience with narrative. But play fosters the ability to practice *authoring* an unfolding narrative. When young children play together, they coauthor an ongoing script that follows strict rules they create.

Just as most readers would put down a nonsensical novel, children will leave a play scenario that is not making sense. To play with others, therefore, one has to learn to follow the rules of making sense in a narrative. While deciphering the written word is a complex and difficult skill to learn, it is even more difficult to learn to appreciate a narrative if one has not received ample practice authoring one. Playing with others creates a foothold for this authorship—and avid readers.

At this school, teachers trust children to play with the powerful ideas involved in superhero play. This environment of trust between the teachers and the children—as well as among the children—is established over months. In such an environment the children can contribute shared ideas about justice and tinker with the nuances of right and wrong. When children and teachers build theories *together* about violence and justice, they directly address the complexities of these topics. And the children are able to do so without judgment or censorship from a teacher who has physical and emotional power over them. Teachers at this school address violence by allowing children to play with this enticing and scary power, using it as a tool for making meaning from their experiences without forcing it into the shadows.

Of course, individual differences must be considered. For some children, pretend acts of violence may elicit strong emotions. In such cases, teachers need to be prepared to reassure children and help them understand that role-play acts of violence are pretend, and that the power a child plays with in a pretend scenario does not have to have "real" consequences. A teacher can, with careful reflection, help all children find ways to participate in play without feeling threatened.

Censorship Creates Underlife

Chen (2009) investigates the hidden *underlife* at school among first-graders, where teacher censorship of certain themes, toys, or actions creates a heightened desire for these things, resulting in toys hidden away in backpacks, under tables, or in restrooms. When these topics are revealed only in secret, there is no possibility for dialogue about the stories they tell and the themes they suggest. But in a curriculum in which pretend violence opens a dialogue about real violence and real-life problem solving, children and teachers can explore the actions that lead the superheroes to choose to fight. Paley describes this freedom as

> democracy at its beginning, and it happens through the genius of make-believe. And yet when we speak about the benefits of . . . early childhood education, we rarely make mention of its superheroes and princesses . . . that which is most urgent to the children and most helps them organize their thoughts. (2012)

The teachers at Eli's school recognize this urgency, and in allowing superhero play they sow the seeds of democratic participation. They also create an opportunity to aid children in organizing their thoughts about violence and justice. Teachers invite themes that are often relegated to the underlife, celebrate them for how desirable they are to the children, and riff on them as a form of creative dialogue (St. John 2010; Kinard & Gainer 2012).

Riffing: Uncensored Play Creates Opportunities to Cocreate

St. John (2010) describes *riffing* as a way to reinterpret old themes and create new themes and motifs from shared narratives. When one jazz musician riffs off another, she uses a fine-tuned ear to make variations on melodies, progressions, and intervals that she and the other musicians share as a common language. These improvised variations are bursts of creativity based on shared connoisseurship (Kinard & Gainer 2012).

Memo to: Preschool Teachers Everywhere
From: Stefanie Adamson-Kain
Date: January 2015
Subject: Children Need and Have a Right to Play

Play is often viewed as what we do after we work. A reward. In most cases, first you work and then you play. Many people work so that they can afford to play (vacations, golf club memberships, electronic games).

However, play is the work of young children. It comes naturally to all children, all over the world. Children are born to play. Play allows children time to investigate, think, create, socialize, question, and problem solve, without judgment from adults.

Play involves risk. What will happen if I step here? What will she do if I tell her no? How do these things fit together? Why isn't this working the way I want it to? Is there another way?

Play provides practice of adult roles. It allows children to express themselves as artists, mathematicians, scientists, athletes, readers, writers, caregivers, leaders, and so much more. It builds confidence so that children will feel comfortable as they encounter challenges throughout their lives.

Play can be rule oriented. Sometimes the play itself dictates the rules. Sometimes it is the children who make the rules. Other times the teacher facilitates the play, using games and playful activities in the learning process.

Play is prior knowledge expressed actively. Children demonstrate their learning through play. Teachers must watch and listen carefully to unlock the play's meaning. Through play, children tell the stories of their lives.

Play creates happiness and balance in life. Without play, how can you discover who you are? Who you want to be? How things work? Play allows children to develop into motivated explorers ready to take on the world.

Stefanie Adamson-Kain, MEd, is a kindergarten teacher at the Center for Young Children on the University of Maryland College Park campus.

When I speak with Leandra, whose painting transforms the children into superheroes, she describes her own connoisseurship:

> I'm a *huge* comic book nerd! I love all of the superheroes and stuff that the children are so into. And the love we share for them is key—we use it to create new characters and new ideas. We love the old scenarios too, but then we create new worlds inside those, where superheroes care about feelings as much as they do about justice.

Sutterby (2009) describes the uneasiness adults have with certain types of play. He defines superhero-themed play and other types as generally being considered bad play by adults. Educators like Hoffman (2004) acknowledge children's desires to play superhero-themed games, but he coaches parents and teachers in ways to segue superhero play into more peaceful play.

Leandra balances the tension many early childhood educators feel. In her role as play coach, Leandra does not place a value on the types of themes the children choose. She does not dictate what others' needs are, nor how to help others. She does not lead the children's thinking away from solving the problems of their plots in ways that make sense to them. She does not coach them toward conforming to her own set of values. She does not censor the tools or actions of the superheroes, only comments on them, offering her perspective as equal to the perspective of anyone else in the circle. She does not define justice. Instead, justice is part of an ongoing dialogue between Leandra's vision and the children's understandings.

For example, as she re-creates the radiating symmetry of Spider-Man's red and black web designs on a child's chest, she asks questions: "Why does Spider-Man use his webs like that?" The children assert that "bad guys have to be stopped!" Some add that webs are gentler than guns. She asks, "Does he ever run out of webs?" The children break into a cacophonous chorus: "I'll make a potion for him that makes new webs!" "No, no. His body makes them!" "We'll feed him new web juice!" "No, I know. We'll give him a shot!" "Yeah, I'll be the doctor!" Teacher and children become an improvisational jazz ensemble. They share ideas as well as a love of the characters and themes, immersing themselves in the creative process.

"Without adult support, the play of many children is destined to never reach [a] fully developed status" (Leong & Bodrova 2015, 27). The play becomes richer and more critically focused when teachers contribute to the planning and preparation of props and scenarios. If children have difficulty coming up with ideas for engaging in free-form pretend play, they might benefit from dictating a story or being part of a group storytelling activity to generate ideas. They could then rehearse a script with a teacher (Cooper 2009).

Leandra facilitates a prolonged play theme, building on the idea that mature play "lasts for long stretches of time: within one play session for an hour or longer or extending over several play sessions and over several days" (Leong & Bodrova 2015, 28). In her approach, Leandra welcomes the themes of superhero play from the outside world and allows the children to fully explore them. A dialogue between teacher and children as well as among peers has begun, in which riffing off others' themes and ideas creates a space for both creativity and critique.

New Powers Imagined

On a subsequent visit, I find Eli once again painted as a superhero. This time blue waves swirl around his torso, arms, and legs—they represent water. Next to him, a boy's limbs are covered in painted fire. Another child's midsection is covered in clouds with curvy waves of wind circling around to his back. A girl's chest is adorned with a thundercloud, a yellow bolt of lightning zigzagging from it. The four of them collect materials to build a hideout and solve problems as Waterman, Fireboy, Windboy, and Thundergirl.

There is still some violence in Eli's play themes. But not only is he playing at pretend violence, he is playing also with the notion of violence—with the idea that superheroes are made-up and that he can imagine the stories in ways that include his teachers' and friends' desires. The themes do not dictate his play actions; he uses the themes to create his own play destiny. After weeks of playing superheroes, Eli and his friends have riffed off Batman's character and, in doing so, have thought deeply and critically about the themes of violence and the two-dimensional characters of the superhero genre. They have created characters like Waterman and Fireboy, who solve problems in novel ways.

Eli merges, hones, remixes, fractures, and cobbles together an array of traits, abilities, and ways of being that he draws from people he knows, stories he's heard, real events, and the artful fantasies of authors, artists, animators, and friends. This mash-up does not blur the line between fantasy and reality. Rather, it provides Eli with the materials for creativity. He tinkers with a concept of self that matches no one human being, but is drawn from all (Leont'ev 1981; Saifer 2010).

It is important that Eli be able to tinker with what scares him and us—the violent side of superheroism. Some educators do allow superhero play, but only if children refrain from pretend violence, never use pretend weapons (even fingers that shoot), and use superpowers only to help others (Hoffman 2004). Such censorship comes from outside the children's control, not as a coauthored approach between teacher and children. The teacher remains the dictator of justice. In contrast to the censoring approach, exploring superheroes by theory building and riffing presents opportunities for children and teachers together to create theories of justice, violence, assistance, access, and privilege through complicated discussions. This is a complex and messy affair.

Conclusion

Becoming a superhero, flying over the school, helps children develop essential skills for later success. But, as Paley (2012) suggests, superhero play is not merely preparation for the future. It is a deep philosophical, psychological, sociological, anthropological exploration of life. It happens in the now, but at the same time it is a sustained, timeless exploration of the human condition. Children and teachers engage in a positive, creative act when they cocreate superhero scenarios. They are not disrupting the classroom community; they are participating in it.

References

Anderson, P.J., & N. Reidy. 2012. "Assessing Executive Function in Preschoolers." *Neuropsychology Review* 22 (4): 345–60.

Bodrova, E., C. Germeroth, & D.J. Leong. 2013. "Play and Self-Regulation: Lessons From Vygotsky." *American Journal of Play* 6 (1): 111–23. www.du.edu/marsicoinstitute/pressroom/6-1-article-play-and-self-regulation.pdf.

Chen, R. 2009. *Early Childhood Identity: Construction, Culture, and the Self.* New York: Peter Lang.

Cooper, P.M. 2009. *The Classrooms All Young Children Need: Lessons in Teaching From Vivian Paley.* Chicago: University of Chicago Press.

Hoffman, E. 2004. *Magic Capes, Amazing Powers: Transforming Superhero Play in the Classroom.* St. Paul, MN: Redleaf.

Kinard, T.A. 2014. "Emotional Learning and Violent Play: Sword Fighting in Summer School." *Early Years* 35 (2): 20–23.

Kinard, T.A., & J.S. Gainer. 2012. "Kissing G.I. Joes: Wide-Awake, Critical Connoisseurship in Critical Media Literacy Pedagogy." *Journal of Curriculum Theorizing* 28 (1): 108–25. http://journal.jctonline.org/index.php/jct/article/view/283/09kinard.pdf.

Leong, D.J., & E. Bodrova. 2015. "Assessing and Scaffolding Make-Believe Play." In *Spotlight on Young Children: Exploring Play*, eds. H. Bohart, K. Charner, & D. Koralek, 26–36. Washington, DC: NAEYC.

Leont'ev, A.N. 1981. *Problems of the Development of the Mind.* 4th ed. Moscow: Progress.

Lillard, A.S., M.D. Lerner, E.J. Hopkins, R.A. Dore, E.D. Smith, & C.M. Palmquist. 2013. "The Impact of Pretend Play on Children's Development: A Review of the Evidence." *Psychological Bulletin* 139 (1): 1–34.

McClelland, M.M., C.E. Cameron, S.B. Wanless, & A. Murray. 2007. "Executive Function, Behavioral Self-Regulation, and Social-Emotional Competence: Links to School Readiness." Chap. 4 in *Contemporary Perspectives on Social Learning in Early Childhood Education,* eds. O.N. Saracho & B. Spodek, 83–107. Charlotte, NC: Information Age.

Obradović, J., X.A. Portilla, & W.T. Boyce. 2012. "Executive Functioning and Developmental Neuroscience: Current Progress and Implications for Early Childhood Education." Chap. 16 in *Handbook of Early Childhood Education,* eds. R.C. Pianta, W.S. Barnett, L.M. Justice, & S.M. Sheridan, 324–51. New York: Guilford.

Paley, V.G. 1988. *Bad Guys Don't Have Birthdays: Fantasy Play at Four.* Chicago: University of Chicago Press.

Paley, V.G. 2004. *A Child's Work: The Importance of Fantasy Play.* Chicago: University of Chicago Press.

Paley, V.G. 2012. "The Beginning of Community: A Nurturing Ground." Keynote speech at the Lady Bird Johnson Centennial Symposium on Early Childhood Education, Texas State University, November 8.

Quintero, E.P. 2009. *Critical Literacy in Early Childhood Education: Artful Story and the Integrated Curriculum.* New York: Peter Lang.

Rimm-Kaufman, S.E., & S.B. Wanless. 2012. "An Ecological Perspective for Understanding the Early Development of Self-Regulatory Skills, Social Skills, and Achievement." Chap. 15 in *Handbook of Early Childhood Education,* eds. R.C. Pianta, W.S. Barnett, L.M. Justice, & S.M. Sheridan, 299–323. New York: Guilford.

Saifer, S. 2010. "Higher Order Play and Its Role in Development and Education." *Psychological Science and Education* (3): 38–50. http://psyjournals.ru/en/psyedu/2010/n3/Saifer.shtml.

St. John, P. 2010. "Crossing Scripts and Swapping Riffs: Preschoolers Make Musical Meaning." Chap. 5 in *Vygotsky and Creativity: A Cultural-Historical Approach to Play, Meaning Making and the Arts,* eds. M.C. Connery, V.P. John-Steiner, & A. Marjanovic-Shane, 63–82. New York: Peter Lang.

Sutterby, J. 2009. "'Bad' Play." In *Encyclopedia of Play in Today's Society, Volume 1,* ed. R.P. Carlisle, 60–61. Thousand Oaks, CA: Sage.

Tough, P. 2009. "The Make-Believe Solution: Can Imaginary Play Teach Children to Control Their Impulses—and Be Better Students?" *New York Times Magazine,* Sept. 27, 31–35. www.nytimes.com/2009/09/27/magazine/27tools-t.html?pagewanted=all.

Vygotsky, L.S. 1978. *Mind in Society: The Development of Higher Psychological Processes.* Ed. and trans. M. Cole, V. John-Steiner, S. Scribner, & E. Souberman. Cambridge, MA: Harvard University Press.

Ysaaca Axelrod

"Todos Vamos a Jugar, Even the Teachers"—Everyone Playing Together

In a bilingual (Spanish and English) 4-year-olds' classroom, Jasmin turns to Soraya and says, "Let's do Michael Jackson." Soraya responds, "Yeah, let's do that." She turns and yells across the room, *"Javier, tú vas a cantar y bailar Michael Jackson"* [Javier, you are going to sing and dance Michael Jackson]. Several of the other children in the room cheer and move chairs around to create an audience. They then invite their friends and the teachers: *"Ven, vamos a hacer un concierto con Michael Jackson"* [Come, we are going to make a Michael Jackson concert]. Massiel, one of the teachers, smiles and says, *"Wow, vamos a ver a Michael Jackson!"* [Wow, we are going to see Michael Jackson!]

After all the children and teachers are seated, applauding, and chanting "Michael Jackson!," Javier puts on a hat and struts onto the stage. He starts dancing and singing "Beat It." The children applaud and Alexander stands up and says, *"Ahora yo"* [Now me]. He starts dancing and singing in Spanish to a reggaeton song, and his classmates cheer. He responds, *"Ya, ya"* [Stop, stop], blushes, and runs off the stage. The children continue to cheer and applaud, and Javier comes back and repeats his previous act.

As quickly as the children assembled for the concert, they move the chairs to different areas of the classroom and play with different items and story lines. But, around the room children and teachers are humming or singing softly "Beat It."

naeyc® 2, 3

Doing Michael Jackson is a recurring theme in this class, although it is unclear how this story line began. Michael Jackson died a few months before the children adopted this theme, and it is quite common to hear his music playing on the streets of the children's New York City neighborhood. Javier, who is familiar with several of Michael Jackson's songs as well as his dance moves, is often called on to play the role of Michael Jackson. The concert story line does not lead to long play episodes; often it takes less than 10 minutes. However, it brings most of the children and teachers together, then dissolves as children move across the room to engage in other kinds of play.

The stories in the children's play flow together and apart as the children move around the room, joining other children or finding an object that catches their attention. The teachers too move in and out of the play, usually invited or drawn in by the children. An observer might notice the constant movement of the children, objects, and teachers. No child remains for very long in any one place or with any single story line, yet a closer look reveals a flow of stories that build on one another, bringing characters in and out, allowing children to step in and out of stories, and bringing with them the richness of their language and cultural practices.

It is not just that the child must make his knowledge his own, but that he must make it his own in a community of those who share his sense of belonging to a culture.

In this article I describe my observations of young emergent bilingual children in a Head Start classroom. I use the term *emergent bilingual* because it honors children's home languages and recognizes that they are developing their home languages as well as English (García 2009). The schedule called for children to spend most of the day engaged in long periods of play (about an hour each, indoors and outdoors), followed by small groups, group meetings, meals, and naptime. I visited the classroom two or three times a week for a year to learn about the children's language and literacy development. My observations and field notes focused on their language practices during play, how they used and negotiated language with their peers, and their language development over the course of the year. I looked at the ways in which play, supported by the teachers, created spaces and opportunities for the children to share and develop language and cultural practices that are important to their sense of identity.

The Importance of Play

Play, once a staple of all early childhood classrooms, has been pushed out of most elementary schools, and we are starting to see this trend in preschool settings (Genishi & Dyson 2009; Nicolopoulou 2010). Early childhood researchers and educators agree that play is key to early childhood development. Through play, young children learn essential skills across all domains (language and literacy, cognitive, physical, and socioemotional) (Van Hoorn et al. 2015). Yet, despite agreement on the importance of play, there is no single agreed-on definition of play, and there are a variety of theories that inform our understanding of play and its development (Saracho 2012). In this article, I focus on Lev Vygoskty's and Jerome Bruner's work on play.

Ysaaca Axelrod, EdD, is an assistant professor of early childhood education at the College of Education at University of Massachusetts, Amherst. A former kindergarten teacher, Ysaaca's work focuses on the language and literacy development of young emergent bilinguals.

For Vygostky (1978), the defining characteristic of play is a child-created imaginary situation. Children invent rules of behavior (including language), often establishing them as the play unfolds. The rules are often dictated by the situations and themes established; for example, during house play children follow familiar behaviors, which they know from their own family or other experiences (e.g., books, movies). "Play creates a zone of proximal development" (102) in which children are able to behave and act in ways that are beyond their age and usual behaviors. Children explore and take on roles they might not usually fill, such as being Michael Jackson in a concert arena.

The work of Bruner (1986) extends Vygotsky's ideas by focusing on the sociocultural aspects of play. He argues that through play children learn about social behaviors, cultural practices, and ways of communicating with others. Bruner believes that play itself is more important than the outcomes; that is, the process of playing is what is important for children more than an end product or goal. For the children playing Michael Jackson, the process of creating the concert and the ease with which the children move on to other play areas demonstrate that for them the concert is not the end goal, but part of the flow in their play.

Vygotsky and Bruner are particularly relevant as we think about classrooms with linguistically and culturally diverse children. Bruner writes, "It is not just that the child must make his knowledge his own, but that he must make it his own in a community of those who share his sense of belonging to a culture" (127). Children intimately influence—and are influenced by—the contexts in which they develop. The children in this Head Start classroom speak Spanish, Mixteco (an indigenous language from Mexico), and Caribbean English in their homes. They live in a predominantly Mexican and Dominican neighborhood in New York City, attend a bilingual classroom with teachers from the Dominican Republic and Argentina, and live in the United States, where English is an unofficial first language. The children daily negotiate multiple languages and cultural practices as well as individual differences and preferences. Yet, through the teachers' thoughtful planning and engagement with the children, the play in this classroom supports each child's development and learning as a cultural being.

Through the teachers' thoughtful planning and engagement with the children, the play in this classroom supports each child's development and learning as a cultural being.

Play With Culturally and Linguistically Diverse Children

The intersection between play and language has led scholars to discuss the role of play in language development (Vygotsky 1986). In sociodramatic play, children must work together to create the fantasy world that they are playing within. Several studies show the ways children negotiate multiple languages and cultures in their play, and how these support their language development. In their article describing three ethnographic studies of emergent bilinguals playing, Long, Volk, and Gregory (2007) describe how through play "children drew from multiple schemas as they co-constructed new spaces and practice for teaching and learning about language, literacy, and cultural roles and routines" (239). In each of these studies, what emerged was "sociocultural common ground" (Dyson 2003, 9)—the children created new meanings by blending together their home and school experiences and languages.

Riojas-Cortez (2001) examines how Mexican American preschoolers draw on their funds of knowledge during sociodramatic play in their classroom. She argues that play is a valuable way for children to bring in elements (language, cultural behaviors) from their home world so that they "can actually observe culture" (35). Because the focus of her study is on how the children incorporate aspects of their Mexican culture into their play, Riojas-Cortez categorizes their use of Spanish as an element of culture. She includes *code-switching* (when a speaker alternates between languages or language varieties)—for example, the use of the word *mija* (an abbreviation of *mi hija*, which means *my daughter*) when speaking in English—as a cultural practice, as does Paugh (2005).

In her work with young emergent bilinguals, Genishi examines the way play creates opportunities for children to learn language and move into classroom activities and play episodes at their own pace (see Genishi & Dyson 2009). A play-based curriculum lets children slowly ease into play with their classmates as they develop language and interactional skills: "[The children] illustrate the cultural universal of play as a means for entering into a shared social life with other children" (64).

These studies show that play provides opportunities for children to negotiate which language to use when and with whom, and to blend their multiple languages and cultural practices. Children also make sense of the different cultures they bring with them to their classrooms and play settings. For children learning multiple languages and dialects, sociodramatic play in particular lets them use their developing languages.

Implications for Practice

While many agree that play is the work of children, Vivian Paley raises a more important point: "Why not call play the work of teachers as well?" (2004, 3). One challenge for early childhood teachers is to find ways to integrate play meaningfully into their classroom curriculum to help support children's development of skills. This is especially important in this era of increased accountability when, in some schools, measurement and assessment drive curricular practices (Genishi & Dyson 2009). Play, which is flexible, unpredictable, collaborative, and ever changing, does not lend itself to the narrow measures used to gauge academic development. It may be hard for some teachers and families to recognize the myriad skills that children develop as they play. However, a close examination of children's play reveals that much of what children are accomplishing and learning through play meets many of the standards in the Head Start Child Development and Early Learning Framework (HHS 2011).

Another challenge for teachers is finding ways to integrate themselves into children's play while supporting and maintaining the integrity of the play and ensuring that it is authentic and meaningful for children. Viviana and Massiel, the teachers in the 4-year-olds' classroom, spend most of the day playing with the children. They are quickly invited or integrated into the children's play.

Soraya: (to Viviana, a teacher) You want me to do your *pelo* [hair]?

Viviana: Ummm, sure.

Soraya takes a plastic spoon from the kitchen area and starts playing with Viviana's hair.

Jasmin: My mami went to the beauty salon and got *rolos* [curlers] last weekend. You want *rolos*?

Viviana: OK.

Massiel: (another teacher, joining in) *Yo tengo que ir a hacerme el pelo* [I have to go get my hair done].

Jasmin: Want me to do it?

Massiel: How much are you going to charge me?

Jasmin: Not much.

Soraya: A lot. My mami says it costs her a lot to do her hair. She does my hair and my sister's hair. She did it with the *plancha* [flatiron] last week, you remember? It was nice.

Viviana: I sometimes do that too.

Soraya: Want me to do the *plancha* now?

Viviana: Not today. Today I am getting *rolos*.

We see the children drawing on their home experiences while getting their hair done in this example, and finding ways to create these scenes in the home area. The teachers are invited to join in, and do so in ways that are congruent with the play, and they draw on their own experiences at the beauty salon. The teachers use the same code-switching patterns as the children, referring to particular items (curlers, flatiron) in Spanish. While the teachers might use this opportunity to teach the children the names of these items in English, instead they use the language that the children use to honor the children's language practices.

The children often speak Spanish, their home language, in the home area of the classroom, where they are more familiar with the Spanish words for items typically found in their homes. The teachers allow for flexible language practices so children can draw from their full linguistic repertoire and practice and play with languages as they develop.

As Vygotsky (1978) states, children use play to try out roles that they are not able to play in real life: doctor, chef, superhero, beautician, mom, and dad. Through children's play we get glimpses into their lives and experiences outside school, and the ways they make sense of their experiences and learn how to be members of society. The teachers in this classroom use play to get to know the children and support their learning. They add objects and items to play areas based on the children's play and conversations. For example, following the beauty salon's appearance, they add a cash register so children can include business transactions to their store and beauty salon play.

Several classroom families are welcoming new babies. For the children who are about to become siblings for the first time, the teachers add baby items such as bottles, diapers, softcover books, and a baby carrier to the home area to help them learn about caring for babies. The teachers include real items with writing in English and Spanish, such as boxes of food the children are familiar with. They add local supermarket circulars, menus from neighborhood restaurants, cell phones, cameras, and other items to the home area that are important and present in the children's lives.

A favorite play event in this class is planning a trip and going on an airplane to the Dominican Republic or Mexico (this varies depending on the leader's home country). The children move the chairs to create rows as in an airplane. The teachers add travel items (such as luggage and used boarding passes) to support the children's play. In addition to their frequent trips to their home countries, the children build computers to Skype with their grandparents and families living abroad. The teachers foster these play events by asking the children about their real and pretend conversations with their grandparents.

They build on the children's transnational experiences and share their own experiences talking to distant loved ones.

The teachers draw on their own life experiences to join the children in play. Some experiences, such as going to the beauty salon or traveling to see family members, are familiar to the teachers; others they learn about from the children. The role of teacher–learner is often reversed in play—the teachers learn from the children, and the children learn from each other. Most of the children and teachers in the class are Latino, and Spanish is the shared language; yet there are some clear cultural and linguistic differences, depending on countries of origin. Play gives children and teachers opportunities to learn more about each other's cultural practices.

Families and Play

When I taught kindergarten, many parents asked why I had play areas in the classroom. They felt that their children came to school to "learn," not play. Sadly, our society has created a dichotomy between play and academic work; in reality, play is an important vehicle for young children to learn. Invite families into the classroom to watch children play, and talk about the skills they are developing. Provide specific examples of how their play supports learning—for example, block play supports spatial development and problem-solving skills, both of which are key to mathematics.

Share these suggestions with families about participating in their children's play:

- Have fun! As an adult you may feel uncomfortable participating in your children's play, but doing so can help you better understand their thinking and emotions, support their language development, introduce new concepts, and support a variety of important skills that will help their social, emotional, and academic growth.
- Observe and listen to how and what children are playing. To play with children in ways that are engaging and authentic for them, know what they like to play. What scenarios do they often act out? What characters do they like to play? What themes do they enjoy?
- Respect children's play choices and characters. While you might wonder about the appropriateness of some of their themes or games (e.g., fighting with pretend swords or building with blocks and then knocking them over), follow their lead and let them decide the rules and form of the play. Play offers a safe way for children to explore their ideas and provides important learning opportunities. Forbidding particular themes or games is usually not effective. Instead, consider offering suggestions for the play that build on the theme. If a "princess" says she is going to use her magic wand to make everyone else ugly, you might suggest that instead she use the wand to give each person a special (positive) power. Listening to and observing children will help you support their play episode instead of discouraging it.
- Recognize that while children's play often has aspects of fantasy, it is usually grounded in real experiences, stories, movies, and other aspects of their lives. Draw on your own experiences to contribute to your child's play episodes. For example, if you are making mangú, talk to your child about measuring the ingredients, following the steps in the process, and so on. These skills might find their way into your child's play the next time his or her superhero character is hungry or your child wants to play restaurant.
- Be flexible and recognize that children's play does not always proceed the way adults would expect; themes and scenarios arise and quickly move into new ones. Offer an occasional suggestion. If your child is playing barber and a "customer" is accidently injured with a pair of scissors, suggest a visit to the "doctor's" office.

Alexander: (to Viviana) *¿Tu quiere hace' mangú?* [Do you want to make mangú?]

Viviana: *Yo no sé como se hace.* [I don't know how to make it.]

Alexander: *Yo te enseño, se hace hacien'o así.* [I will show you, you make it like this.]

Alexander makes mashing motions in a bowl, putting a lot of effort into it and muttering. *Así, así, y ma' así.* [Like this, like this, and more like this.] *Ya casi.* [Almost ready.]

Viviana: *¿Pero que tienes que hacer?* [What do you need to do?]

Alexander: *¿No me estaba' viendo? Así, así, y luego lo cocina' con carne y arro'.* [Weren't you watching me? Like this, like this, and then you cook it with meat and rice.]

Viviana: Ahhhhhh.

Aurora: (a nearby teacher) *Yo voy a tener que ir a tu casa pa que tu me haga' mangú, po'que eso suena bien rico.* [I am going to have to go to your house so that you can make me mangú, because that sounds very delicious.]

Alexander: (smiles and blushes) No, no, no.

Luna: *Yo no sé lo que es mangú.* [I don't know what mangú is.]

Javier: Mangú is like mango?

Alexander wags his finger vigorously no.

Aurora: (laughs) *No, no, mangú es plátano.* [Mangú is from plantains.]

Luna and Javier: Ahhhhhh.

Alexander and his family are from the Dominican Republic and maintain strong ties to and pride in their Dominican heritage, including making a popular plantain dish called *mangú*, which is a favorite of Alexander's. Viviana is familiar with mangú, but it is not part of her Argentinian cuisine. In this episode, the role of teacher–learner is reversed as Alexander teaches Viviana how to mash the plantains for this dish. He even shows slight exasperation when she doesn't pay close enough attention. Luna and Javier (both from Mexico) join the conversation and, because of their unfamiliarity with mangú, confuse the word with mango, which they are familiar with. Luna and Javier learn a new word and a new dish from their classmate.

These conversations occur frequently during play as the children bring in elements and experiences from home. Some are shared; others are new and unfamiliar. Differences lead to conversations, and children and teachers learn from each other. Play allows children to take on new roles and take risks with characters, roles, and language (Long, Volk, & Gregory 2007). Play expands the classroom setting to include the fantasy worlds that the children create and communicate in.

Strategies for Teachers

Play should be a cornerstone of early childhood education. The stories from this classroom show how teachers support culturally and linguistically diverse children through a play-based curriculum that honors their languages and cultural practices. Because each classroom is unique, the suggestions that follow are key elements of a philosophy that fosters play and supports children and teachers.

Provide time and space for play. The schedule in this classroom offers children long periods of play. They move around the classroom throughout their play and mix items across play areas. There are no limitations to how many children can be in any area. This freedom allows them to move around, join different stories, and create collective stories, such as the Michael Jackson concert and the Dominican Republic trip. This flexibility allows for story continuity. As children gain language and experiences, they refine and evolve their stories.

Listen to children. It's a common early childhood practice to include items from children's cultures in play areas, such as culturally specific kitchen items, food, and clothing. While items are important, it is also vital to listen to children and become aware of what is significant to them, their families, and the local culture. The children who live in the neighborhood are familiar with the supermarket and local eateries. Menus and circulars from these places are part of the children's lives and experiences outside of the classroom.

Many stories that are important to the children are not always cultural in the traditional sense of being tied to their heritage. The stories are part of their current experiences—becoming an older sibling, traveling to see family members, getting ready for a new school. When teachers sit and listen to children, they can use what they learn to develop a play environment that incorporates specific aspects of the children's lives.

Join children in play. The teachers are welcome and skillful players who follow the children's lead and do not try to change or shift stories. Instead, they engage with the children as cultural beings, bringing in their own language practices and experiences. They observe and learn more about the children while playing with them. The information they gain about the children's interests helps them add items to the play areas to foster stories and create lessons for small or whole group activities.

Conclusion

Jones and Reynolds write, "In their play, children invent the world for themselves and create a place for themselves in it. . . . Teachers need to pay attention to play" (2011, 133). As our schools become increasingly diverse, this is even more relevant. These Head Start teachers use the children's play to learn about the children, their lives, and what is meaningful to them. They learn how best to scaffold children's knowledge of the world through purposeful planning of play environments and engaging with the children. They are important players, with elements of cultural and linguistic diversity coming from the children's and teachers' experiences. Together they negotiate and navigate their differences in ways that foster respect and honor diversity.

References

Bruner, J. 1986. *Actual Minds, Possible Worlds.* Cambridge, MA: Harvard University Press.

Dyson, A.H. 2003. *The Brothers and Sisters Learn to Write: Popular Literacies in Childhood and School Cultures.* New York: Teachers College Press.

García, O. 2009. *Bilingual Education in the 21st Century: A Global Perspective.* Malden, MA: Wiley-Blackwell.

Memo to: Staff in State Departments of Education
From: Linda Espinosa
Date: January 2015
Subject: Play and Language

Mastering the features of any language is challenging and takes years for all children; learning two or more languages during the early childhood years can be especially challenging. It takes frequent opportunities to hear and practice the specific features and vocabulary of a language. In addition, children must be motivated to struggle through the inevitable mistakes and miscommunications. For dual language learners, play provides an excellent context for practicing their new language and making friends across languages.

Young children will work tirelessly to learn a language so they can join in others' play. When they engage in role playing, or imaginative play, or outdoor games and exploration, they naturally take risks with language and accept each other's contributions. As dual language learners practice and acquire language in this highly motivating supportive setting, they can use their skills more independently and in a wider variety of contexts. Communicating and making choices in play helps children develop confidence, build relationships, and negotiate and resolve conflicts, increasing their feelings of success with the new language.

Play also promotes the development of symbolic representation, leading to the development of oral language skills and, later, written language. Thus, play is an excellent context for language learning.

Linda Espinosa, PhD, is co-principal investigator on a project at the University of Chicago and former professor of early childhood education at the University of Missouri, Columbia.

Genishi, C., & A.H. Dyson. 2009. *Children, Language, and Literacy: Diverse Learners in Diverse Times.* New York: Teachers College Press; Washington, DC: NAEYC.

HHS (US Department of Health and Human Services). 2011. *The Head Start Child Development and Early Learning Framework: Promoting Positive Outcomes in Early Childhood Programs Serving Children 3–5 Years Old.* Washington, DC: HHS. http://eclkc.ohs.acf.hhs.gov/hslc/tta-system/teaching/eecd/Assessment/Child%20Outcomes/HS_Revised_Child_Outcomes_Framework(rev-Sept2011).pdf.

Jones, E., & G. Reynolds. 2011. *The Play's the Thing: Teachers' Roles in Children's Play.* 2nd ed. New York: Teachers College Press.

Long, S., D. Volk, & E. Gregory. 2007. "Intentionality and Expertise: Learning From Observations of Children at Play in Multilingual, Multicultural Contexts." *Anthropology & Education Quarterly* 38 (3): 239–59.

Nicolopoulou, A. 2010. "The Alarming Disappearance of Play From Early Childhood Education." *Human Development* 53 (1): 1–4.

Paley, V.G. 2004. *A Child's Work: The Importance of Fantasy Play.* Chicago: University of Chicago Press.

Paugh, A.L. 2005. "Multilingual Play: Children's Code-Switching, Role Play, and Agency in Dominica, West Indies." *Language in Society* 34 (1): 63–86.

Riojas-Cortez, M. 2001. "Preschoolers' Funds of Knowledge Displayed Through Sociodramatic Play Episodes in a Bilingual Classroom." *Early Childhood Education Journal* 29 (1): 35–40.

Saracho, O.N. 2012. *An Integrated Play-Based Curriculum for Young Children.* New York: Routledge.

Van Hoorn, J., P.M. Nourot, B. Scales, & K.R. Alward. 2015. *Play at the Center of the Curriculum.* 6th ed. Upper Saddle River, NJ: Pearson.

Vygotsky, L.S. 1978. *Mind in Society: The Development of Higher Psychological Processes.* Ed. and trans. M. Cole, V. John-Steiner, S. Scribner, & E. Souberman. Cambridge, MA: Harvard University Press.

Vygotsky, L.S. 1986. *Thought and Language.* Rev. ed. Ed. A. Kozulin. Cambridge, MA: MIT Press.

Jeffrey Trawick-Smith, Jennifer Wolff, Marley Koschel, and Jamie Vallarelli

Which Toys Promote High-Quality Play? Reflections on the Five-Year Anniversary of the TIMPANI Study

Lealem looks over a new set of toys she will introduce in her preschool classroom. Rainbow people—two dozen multicolored wooden people with no features—stand at attention on a table. "I wonder what kinds of play these toys will inspire," she says to Jeffrey as he prepares to study how children will use them during choice time. "What will the children do with them?"

During choice time many children use them and do so in different ways. Four-year-old boys Jim and Emir approach the table where these toys are displayed and engage in a pretend-play theme. Jim selects a yellow figure and explains that it is the creature who will capture all the other figures. Emir manipulates the other pieces, pretending that they are running away. "Let's say he eats up all of these guys," announces Jim, the child doing the chasing. He then growls frighteningly. Emir cries, "Run, run, as fast as you can!" He herds all of the other wooden people to a corner of the table and says, "He can't get them here, all right? They're in the apartment and the doors are locked." The play continues for several minutes.

Later, 5-year-old Melly goes to the table by herself. She pulls all four chairs away from the table and lines them up in a row. She then places the wooden people in lines on each of the chairs. "They're watching a movie," Melly says to Lealem as she passes by. The teacher notices that all the red people are lined up on one chair, all the blue on another, and so on. The activity is brief, but the child is completely engaged in the play.

naeyc® 2, 3

On the same day, 4-year-old Amy and 5-year-old Hana discover that they can stack the colorful people on top of each other. For a few minutes they build tall and precarious towers with the toys. Then they stand back, admiring their work. Amy claps with delight and calls a teacher over: "Look what we made! Please take a picture!"

Near the end of choice time, two 3-year-old boys wander by the table, briefly look at the toys, handle them, then move on to another area of the classroom, seemingly uninterested.

Observing these different interactions, Lealem and Jeffrey ask themselves, "What exactly is the impact of these toys on play? Some children pretend with them, while others use them to sort or build. Some children interact with peers while using them; others play alone. Some don't play with the toys at all."

With such a diversity of children's responses to a single play material, can we really say that this or any other toy is beneficial for *all* children in preschool classrooms? For five years, the Center for Early Childhood Education at Eastern Connecticut State University has been struggling with this question. Students and I conduct an annual toy study called TIMPANI (Toys That Inspire Mindful Play and Nurture the Imagination) for several reasons. Such research is important and provides practical information for teachers. The quality of children's play in preschool predicts later social and intellectual development (Vygotsky 1976), and a large percentage of classroom play includes toys. However, toys have received little research attention. Preschool teachers need empirical evidence to guide the decisions they make about which toys to provide in their classrooms.

On the fifth anniversary of our project, we reflect on toys and summarize some of the big ideas drawn from our findings. Preschool teachers may find them useful as they choose new play materials for their classrooms.

Jeffrey Trawick-Smith, EdD, holds the Phyllis Waite Endowed Chair in Early Childhood Education at Eastern Connecticut State University. He has conducted numerous studies on young children's play and cultural diversity in early childhood development.

Jennifer Wolff, BS, served as a research assistant at Eastern and is a preschool teacher in the New Britain, Connecticut, public school system.

Marley Koschel, BS, was a research assistant at Eastern and is a graduate assistant and master's degree student at Wheelock College in Boston.

Jamie Vallarelli, BS, was a research assistant at Eastern and is a kindergarten teacher in the Windham, Connecticut, public school system.

What Are Toys and Why Do We Study Them?

We consider toys to be any concrete object that children can manipulate to carry out self-directed and meaningful play activities that are enjoyable for the process and not because they result in a product. A toy could be a pretend-play prop, a building material, an art medium, a set of natural objects to explore scientifically, or even a stick. For the purposes of our research, we do not consider computer applications, videos, or books to be toys. Further, we do not study outdoor play equipment because our recording equipment is available only indoors.

Sometimes teachers ask us why we call the things we study *toys*. To some, the term sounds dated. The trend is to use more education-related names when referring to what children play with in classrooms. For example, we have heard puzzles and blocks referred to as *instructional materials*. This may stem from a misconception among some administrators or policy makers that play and all things used in play are unimportant for learning. Some teachers try to assuage these concerns by changing their vocabulary. A kindergarten teacher summarized the problem this way: "I avoid using the *P*-word—*play*. It's just not appreciated anymore. We talk about *learning* centers and *learning* materials and *learning* time. That seems to satisfy everyone." As the articles in this book document, play and what children play with are critical for development. We use the words *toys* and *play* in our research to communicate that they are fundamental aspects of childhood.

Why do we study toys? Toys influence various aspects of children's play. For example, some toys, such as pretend-play props and blocks, prompt more social interaction than other materials both in children with disabilities and those without (Kasari, Freeman, & Paparella 2006; Elmore & Vail 2011). Some toddlers and young preschoolers may need highly realistic props to engage in pretend play at all, whereas older preschoolers often engage in more symbolic make-believe with nonrealistic objects such as blocks, nondescript rubber shapes, or paper towel rolls (Trawick-Smith 1993). A number of studies show that boys and girls often choose different, and sometimes gender-stereotyped, toys to play with (Cherney & Dempsey 2010; Francis 2010). These intriguing findings have led us to conduct our TIMPANI studies on a broad range of toys and to examine their impact on many different aspects of play.

Determining Quality of Play

What do we look for when we rate a toy? We assign the toy a score for each of the following dimensions of play:

- Does a child using the toy demonstrate **thinking and learning behaviors**, such as exploring objects, displaying facial expressions of deep concentration, and commenting on new concepts or discoveries?
- Does the child engage in **problem solving** with the toy, such as trying to overcome challenging obstacles and completing difficult tasks?
- Does the child show **curiosity** when playing with the toy, such as asking questions about its properties and uses or showing facial expressions of puzzlement or fascination?
- Does the child show **sustained interest**, such as persisting in play with the toy with minimal distraction?
- Does the child engage in **creative expression**, such as using the toy in a novel way or conveying unique ideas?
- Does the child enact **symbolic transformations**, such as using the toy to represent something completely different and engaging in pretend play?
- Does the child **collaborate and communicate** with peers when playing with the toy?
- Can the child **use the toy independently** without expressions of frustration or the need for adult assistance?

How We Study Toys

Each year we ask parents, teachers, university faculty, and college students to nominate toys they would like us to study. We ask them to identify toys they believe are developmentally beneficial and enjoyable. Because types of toys vary depending on the manufacturer, we ask people to identify the specific brands of the toys they nominate. We screen the toys to eliminate any that are inappropriate for preschoolers—for example, board games that are too difficult for young children, war toys, or commercial action figures related to popular television programs or movies.

We then place each toy in four different preschool classrooms serving children and families of diverse cultural and socioeconomic backgrounds. We video record children's natural play with each toy for three days in each classroom, for a total of 240 hours of video. Two of us independently view the videos and rate each toy according to the quality of children's play, using a rating system developed in a previous research project (Trawick-Smith, Russell, & Swaminathan 2011). (See "Determining Quality of Play.") The two raters always have a high level of agreement in rating the toys. We then use a series of statistical analyses to determine whether differences in scores between the toys we studied are significant—that is, whether they are beyond what we would expect by chance.

We use the words *toys* and *play* in our research to communicate that they are fundamental aspects of childhood.

TIMPANI Findings: Five Years of Toy Research

After studying toys for five years, we have identified toys that score high and low on our rating system. We have rarely found a toy that inspires high-quality play for all children

all the time. Our most important finding, however, is that the impact of a particular toy on children's play is varied and complex. This is illustrated by the play with the rainbow people in the opening vignette. The children played with these figures in many different ways. The effect of the figures on the quality of children's play varied according to children's backgrounds and characteristics. From our studies we have drawn five important conclusions about toys that have implications for teachers of young children.

1. Children don't always choose to play with toys that inspire the highest-quality play.

A teacher we interviewed explained that she included certain toys in her classroom because "children absolutely love them." Although this is an important dimension of a toy, children's toy preferences and a toy's impact on play are two different things. Every year we identify toys that have positive effects on the quality of play but are rarely chosen by children during choice time. Alternatively, we always find toys that are less likely to promote high-quality play but are very popular. The rainbow people exemplify this finding. They were one of the highest-scoring toys for quality of play in the year we studied them, but children chose them less frequently than any other toy.

Implications for teachers. Careful observation of what children do with toys reveals their impact on play. Through observation, teachers can identify toys that children choose often and that also inspire high-quality play. In our research, large interlocking construction blocks and a wooden train set are examples of such toys. Many children were drawn to these toys and engaged in very high-quality play when using them.

Teachers might also learn that popular toys may have a less positive impact on play. However, through asking questions, modeling, and scaffolding play activities, teachers might enrich play with such toys. Some toys may promote high-quality play but are rarely used. Teachers might encourage more frequent play with such toys by introducing them with enthusiasm at group time, placing them in more prominent locations in the classroom, and modeling their use during choice time.

A toy that is novel and engaging to a child with one set of experiences may be less inspiring to a child with different experiences.

One other possible outcome of toy observation is that a toy may be neither used often nor supportive of quality play. Our research suggests that such toys exist—including some that are commonly found in preschools. Teachers can remove these toys from the classroom altogether or reintroduce them later in the year as children grow older and develop new skills and interests that are matches for those toys. Teachers can also try them again with another group in another year. Giving up on toys that have long been included in one's classroom can be difficult, but it may be necessary for some toys and some groups of preschoolers. One preschool teacher observed that a beautiful natural wood tea set, which children had played with in her previous classrooms for years, didn't inspire much play in her new, multicultural classroom. Much as she loved these materials, she concluded that they were simply not a part of this group of children's cultural and family experiences.

2. Children of different genders and from diverse backgrounds play with toys in different ways.

One of the most important TIMPANI research findings is that how children play with toys is influenced by age, gender, culture, and socioeconomic status. As shown in the opening vignette, variations in play with rainbow people were highly related to gender and age. One year we found that a Play-Doh set with cutting, shaping, and rolling tools received higher scores on play quality when girls played with it than when boys did. In contrast, a marble run—a set of tracks and marbles—received higher scores when used by boys. Two collections of miniature toy vehicles—a set of wooden cars, trucks, and road signs and a wooden train set—received particularly high scores on play quality when Latino children and children from families with low incomes played with them.

Children of different genders and of diverse cultural and socioeconomic backgrounds may play with fewer or different kinds of toys in their homes. Their play styles and toy preferences may be shaped by their families' cultural beliefs. For example, some families highly value collective, collaborative interactions. Their children might be drawn to toys that inspire higher levels of social participation, such as toy vehicles and pretend-play sets that allow active interactions among many peers. A toy that is novel and engaging to a child with one set of experiences may be less inspiring to a child with different experiences. For example, a child who has played with many different types of construction materials since age 2 may be less excited about a new building set. A child who has had few opportunities to build with construction materials may be especially inspired by these toys.

Implications for teachers. In observing play with toys, teachers may find that some toys inspire higher-quality play for girls than for boys or for children of particular cultural backgrounds. When teachers provide a balance of these toys, children of all cultures and both genders can have access to materials that prompt high levels of play quality. Teacher observations may also reveal a few toys that engender high-quality play for all children in the classroom. Examples from our studies of these universally effective toys include magnetic construction shapes and plastic tools. Identifying and providing such toys for preschoolers not only elevates play quality for all children but also may promote richer cross-gender and cross-cultural play.

Our findings on the effects of toys on the play of children of diverse backgrounds also suggest a need to collaborate with families when choosing materials for the classroom. Teachers might ask families about toys that hold cultural meaning for them. Are there toys that reflect the family's cultural beliefs or practices? What toys did the adults play with when they were children? What toys did older siblings or cousins enjoy playing with? What family experiences do the children enjoy? Teachers can then build on these experiences through the classroom play materials. A study conducted in Puerto Rico revealed that families have keen insights into the kinds of toys that inspire their children's play (Trawick-Smith 2010). In this investigation, families indicated that their children

Families and Play

Years ago I had an enlightening experience with my 5-year-old son during a holiday time. Benjamin received gifts from parents, grandparents, aunts, and uncles. Following the gift opening, there was a full half-hour of quiet as he played happily with his new toys. But as I was cleaning up the holiday dinner dishes, I felt a tug on my pant leg. Benjamin looked up at me and asked, "What can I do?" Really? He was already tired of playing with the sparkling, flashing toys scattered on the living room floor? He had begged for these toys prior to the holiday. His friends all played with them, he had claimed, and he had seen them advertised in flyers in the newspaper. How could he have tired of them so quickly?

My family—like many families—would have benefitted from some guidance in selecting toys for children. Teachers can provide this guidance. Doing so will not only help families use their sometimes-scarce resources to invest in toys that children will enjoy over time but will also help ensure that children's play at home supports their development.

Here are some suggestions to share with families about selecting toys:

- **Select toys because they enhance children's play, not just because children ask for them.** Young children often request toys that have limited play value. They may be initially dazzled by flashy, battery-operated features that do not promote high-quality play and may even inhibit it. Select toys for children in the same way you choose their snacks for them: Pick what is healthy for them, not just what they desire.
- **Remember that basic is better when selecting toys.** Although highly realistic, "some assembly required" toys may be initially attractive to children, basic toys that have many different uses are more beneficial and will engage children for longer periods. Blocks, Legos, or Tinkertoys can be used in numerous ways and promote many different areas of development. A talking telephone or a realistic superhero figure has limited play value.
- **Realize that "educational toys" often aren't.** Be wary of toys that are advertised as promoting academic learning. These claims are often misleading. More important, some of these are not really toys—that is, they do not encourage children to play at all. The greatest academic benefits come from play with toys that inspire make-believe, language, social interaction, and problem solving. A set of unit blocks far surpasses a letter-naming game in its impact on learning.
- **Consider toys that have meaning to your family and culture.** Choose some toys that you yourself played with as a child and that you would enjoy using with your own child. Such toys are likely to be part of your family's culture and traditions. If you played games with your family as a child, you might introduce some of these games to your own child. If you built with blocks, those would be important to provide. Such toys transmit to your child the traditions and history of your family.

often engaged in elaborate family-oriented play with dolls, vehicles, and miniature people—toys not unlike the rainbow people described in the opening vignette. These family insights were borne out in later classroom observations.

Open-ended toys that lead to high-quality play contribute more to academic outcomes than many educational toys.

3. Simple, open-ended toys promote higher-quality play than realistic ones with only one use.

Nearly all of the highest-scoring toys in our rating system have a simple design and can be used in many different ways. For example, children used Tinkertoys—one of our highest-scoring toys one year—to engage in a remarkable number of play activities. Children built various structures, used them as pretend-play props (magic wands and helicopters were particularly prevalent), and made rolling creations for block ramps. We observed one group of children use large interlocking construction blocks—another high-scoring toy—to first build a house and then a cell phone, so the mother in the house could call her children. The uses of such toys are limited only by children's imaginations.

Compare these examples to the way children used a talking telephone. This electronic toy carries on conversations with children and selects a theme for them by asking questions such as, "Do you want to go to the zoo?" It prompted the lowest levels of quality and popular play of any toy in our project.

We also found that so-called educational toys, such as a toy telephone that is supposed to teach language and numbers, do not often inspire high-quality play. These toys often have only one use, whether it is counting, recognizing letters, or naming animals. While children may find them interesting initially, they quickly abandon these toys during choice time. We have concluded that open-ended toys that lead to high-quality play contribute more to academic outcomes than many educational toys.

One simple open-ended toy scored higher than all others across all five years of our study: hardwood unit blocks. This will not surprise experienced preschool teachers. There is a good reason blocks have been a fixture in early childhood classrooms since Caroline Pratt designed them in 1913 (Tunks 2013). Blocks inspire construction, make-believe, artistic expression, motor play, and sorting and categorizing. We also found that children's language and social interactions improved more when playing with unit blocks than with any other toy.

Implications for teachers. These findings suggest that teachers can rely on *simple* and *open-ended* as criteria for selecting toys for the classroom. Teachers might ask, "How many different ways can children play with these toys?" "Will they inspire divergent and imaginative play themes as well as problem-solving activities? Or will they restrict play to a narrow range of behaviors?"

Memo to: Families of Young Children
From: Carol Copple
Date: January 2015
Subject: Play *and* Learning

Do you remember the joys of childhood play? You probably want your children to experience the same sense of joy. And, it's likely you also want them to have the learning and preparation they need to do well in school. Luckily, families of young children don't have to choose between play and learning. There is no better way for children to learn and develop than through play, which has certain defining features.

Play is freely chosen. Children are under no pressure to play and can quit any time.

Play means being in an active, alert, nonstressed frame of mind. Children at play are in the "flow," focused on the activity itself, not a specific goal. This state of mind supports children's creativity and is ideal for learning new skills.

Play is guided by mental rules. It always has structure, which derives from rules in the player's mind.

Play benefits children's physical, cognitive, social, and emotional development. In play, children are relaxed and engaged. They become powerful in their play, unlike in the real world where they are dependent on adults. In play, they are able to build and create. They can take on scary creatures and "bad guys" and vanquish them. Assuming the roles of parents and other grownups, children feel capable and in control. This is pure joy. These experiences also enable children to develop language, learn about the world around them, and practice social skills. They solve problems and negotiate as they play with other children. And, importantly, they learn to regulate their own behavior to continue in the play.

Many toys with high-tech or letter and number features are marketed as "educational." And many organized activities are promoted as giving children a head start on learning. But these materials and experiences very often do not provide the rich benefits of true play. When we make choices for children, we can remember—it's not a matter of play versus learning but of play *and* learning.

Carol Copple, PhD, is an author and early education consultant in Nashville, Tennessee.

4. Some effective toys inspire only one dimension of play; balance across toys is important.

Over the course of the study we have identified toys that were exceptional in inspiring one or several aspects of play, but were far less effective in enhancing play in other areas. For example, wooden puzzles received high scores on three dimensions of our rating system (thinking/learning, problem solving, and sustaining attention) but low scores on creative expression, imagination, and social interaction. In contrast, collage materials received remarkably high ratings on creativity and imagination but relatively low scores on problem solving and social interaction. Teachers may choose to include these materials in their classrooms because they have powerful, if narrower, effects on play. Not all toys inspire play in all areas.

Implications for teachers. We recommend balance across toys so that children are inspired to engage in all critical dimensions of play. When equipping a classroom, teachers might provide a core group of toys that meets most or all play quality criteria and appeals to children of multiple backgrounds and characteristics. These could include, for example, blocks and other construction toys, toy vehicles, and plastic tools. Teachers might then add toys that are effective in enhancing one or more dimensions of play—art materials to promote creative expression; sorting and ordering materials, such as Montessori cylinder blocks, that enhance thinking and problem solving; and dramatic play props to encourage social interaction and language skills.

5. Educators can offer families support in selecting toys for their children.

Many families possess good instincts about which toys their children will play with in meaningful ways (Trawick-Smith 2010); however, families sometimes ask for help in choosing toys. They may be misled by advertisements that make claims about a toy's learning value, uncertain about toys related to movies or television shows, or hesitant about action figures that come with special meals at fast food restaurants. Teachers can provide checklists, post articles, and lead workshops for families about choosing toys that benefit children's development. Teachers might think about holidays and birthdays when they share information. They can also share with individual families their observations of their child's classroom toy use.

Implications for teachers. When talking about toys, teachers should consider costs and guide families to less expensive but equally beneficial options. Many toys that effectively support high-quality play are expensive. However, we have found online relatively inexpensive facsimiles of most of our highest-scoring toys: train sets, wooden vehicles and road signs, smaller sets of interlocking blocks (without elaborate accessories), wooden blocks, and plastic tool sets. As long as the less expensive versions are safe, the toys will work well for play at home where there is less wear on them than in a classroom.

Final Thoughts: The Importance of Being Responsive

Our research has provided insights into the effects of toys on young children's play. It has also raised new questions. Ultimately our study shows that it is important for teachers to consider individual children's needs, skills, and interests when they select toys for their classrooms, just as they respond to individual children's needs in all other aspects of teaching. A single set of toys cannot meet the needs of all children in a classroom year after year. A child with specific interests, a unique temperament, or developmental disabilities, or who is from a particular culture, may require a unique collection of toys to inspire high-quality play. Observations of toy use, experimentation with new materials, and interviews with families help teachers find optimal combinations of toys that support all dimensions of play for all children.

References

Cherney, I.D., & J. Dempsey. 2010. "Young Children's Classification, Stereotyping, and Play Behaviour for Gender Neutral and Ambiguous Toys." *Educational Psychology* 30 (6): 651–69.

Elmore, S.R., & C.O. Vail. 2011. "Effects of Isolate and Social Toys on the Social Interactions of Preschoolers in an Inclusive Head Start Classroom." *NHSA Dialog* 14 (1): 1–15.

Francis, B. 2010. "Gender, Toys, and Learning." *Oxford Review of Education* 36 (3): 325–44.

Kasari, C., S. Freeman, & T. Paparella. 2006. "Joint Attention and Symbolic Play in Young Children With Autism: A Randomized Controlled Intervention Study." *Journal of Child Psychology and Psychiatry* 47 (6): 611–20.

Trawick-Smith, J. 1993. "Effects of Realistic, Nonrealistic, and Mixed Realism Play Environments on Young Children's Symbolization, Social Interaction, and Language." Paper presented at the Annual Meeting of the American Educational Research Association, Atlanta, GA, April.

Trawick-Smith, J. 2010. "Drawing Back the Lens on Play: A Frame Analysis of Young Children's Play in Puerto Rico." *Early Education and Development* 21 (4): 536–67.

Trawick-Smith, J., H. Russell, & S. Swaminathan. 2011. "Measuring the Effects of Toys on the Problem-Solving, Creative, and Social Behaviours of Preschool Children." *Early Child Development and Care* 181 (7): 909–27.

Tunks, K.W. 2013. "Happy 100th Birthday, Unit Blocks!" *Young Children* 68 (5): 82–87.

Vygotsky, L.S. 1976. "Play and Its Role in the Mental Development of the Child." In *Play: Its Role in Development and Evolution*, eds. J.S. Bruner, A. Jolly, & K. Sylva, 537–52. New York: Basic Books.

M. Susan McWilliams, Ashley Brailsford Vaughns, Anne O'Hara, Loretta S. Novotny, and Theodora Jo Kyle

Art Play: Stories of Engaging Families, Inspiring Learning, and Exploring Emotions

> Collage is the ultimate playful technique. . . . When you put it all together, you create something new. It is really about trial and error about trying things and making mistakes. It's about forgiving yourself when you make mistakes, and playfulness lets you do that.
>
> —Hanoch Piven, "Living in a Playful Collage"

Hanoch Piven, an internationally known collage-caricature artist, visited Omaha, Nebraska, to conduct arts-based workshops for families, teachers, and children. The workshops were organized by the Omaha Family Literacy Partnership (OFLP). The partnership promotes literacy learning among children and their families through community activities such as author and illustrator visits, family book celebrations, storytelling events, book distributions, and puppet shows. The OFLP invited Piven, an author and illustrator of children's books, because of his connection to literacy. Playful explorations with objects are his method of creating art, and this method was the focus of the workshops.

The weeklong project engaged more than 2,000 children, teachers, and family members at a number of locations: a children's museum, a nonprofit center for immigrant families, the University of Nebraska Omaha, a public library branch, and local schools that serve pre-K through grade 6 children from families with low incomes. Its success was due in part to the excitement of the teachers,

naeyc® 2, 3, 7

families, and community partners. Success was also contingent on thorough preparation and, of course, on the talent, energy, and communication skills of the visiting artist.

To learn more about Hanoch Piven and his concepts about creating art, watch his engaging TED presentation, "Hanoch Piven: Living in a Playful Collage," at **www.youtube.com/watch?v=6e99DuPQ6j8.**

Art Play

The project focused on literacy, with the theme of play's strong presence in art creation running through the workshops. One result was that participating educators gained a newfound respect for playful art explorations as a strategy for developing literacy learning. Overall, the surprise discovery was that the artwork itself was not the most important outcome of the events. Instead, the true value of the experience was in the interactions and stories that flowed from the playful exploration of materials and process of creating.

Although project participants were not intentionally aligned with the Reggio Emilia experience in early childhood education, we found overlapping areas between the practices of some OFLP partners and several Reggio components. For example, the collages in Piven's children's books brought to mind the Reggio Emilia School project "L' importanza di rivedersi/The importance of seeing yourself again" (Malaguzzi & Musatti 1996). The Hundred Languages of Children exhibit demonstrated how children explored "identity" through a project focused on revisiting the concept of oneself using collage as a mode of expression (or "language" in Reggio terms). Strikingly similar to Piven's art were faces that children in Reggio programs created with recyclable materials. Old fountain pen tips (nibs) became eyes, while noses were symbolized by spoons, forks, and a pair of scissors. A leaf represented a mouth, and feathers made eyebrows.

The term *art play* describes the multiple dimensions and levels of play that occur when children create art. Like make-believe play, narratives, and other meaning-making activities, producing art is a way children make sense of their worlds (Anning & Ring 2004; Kolbe 2005a, 2005b; Ahn & Filipenko 2007; Bhroin 2007; Bentley 2013). Freedom to take risks during play is pivotal to the art as well as the play experience—"children in play can be free to experiment and take risks that they might not take in other circumstances" (Ostroff 2012, 26). Taking risks in art play is part of Hanoch Piven's process.

Art play takes place in a risk-safe classroom culture that supports playful learning. In such classrooms, teachers encourage trial and error, value exploration, and respect children's individual perspectives. Mistakes are an accepted and necessary part of the playing and learning processes. On a play continuum with free play at one end and teacher-guided play at the other, art play with children spans the entire range. Specific adult-imposed goals or agendas are not part of art play found on the free play end of the continuum. Alternatively, at the other end of the continuum—guided play—teachers are integral to the art-play process and learning. Three educators tell their stories in this article.

M. Susan McWilliams, PhD, is an associate professor of teacher education at the University of Nebraska Omaha and director of the Omaha Family Literacy Partnership.

Ashley Brailsford Vaughns, PhD, is an assistant professor of early childhood education at the College of Charleston.

Anne O'Hara is the director of the Learning Community Center of South Omaha.

Loretta S. Novotny, MS, is an inclusive Head Start prekindergarten teacher at Wakonda Elementary for the Omaha Public Schools.

Theodora Jo Kyle, MS, is a migrant and refugee prekindergarten teacher with Omaha Public Schools.

Authors' Note: We wish to thank our Omaha Family Literacy Partnership funders who made this project possible: College of Education at the University of Nebraska Omaha, Omaha Public Schools, Mrs. Carol Gendler, Humanities Nebraska, Nebraska Endowment for the Arts, and Nebraska Arts Council. This article may not necessarily reflect the views of the funders.

Engaging Families

The Learning Community Center of South Omaha helps new immigrant families with English language learning and connects them with services and resources. The center follows a family literacy model to increase educational and literacy levels for both children and their families, and center staff work to establish strong relationships with families. The center offered a family art exploration workshop facilitated by Hanoch Piven.

One hallmark of the Reggio Emilia experience is the importance of family participation in the programs and in the education of their young children. In interviews with Loris Malaguzzi (between 1989 and 1992), Gandini (2012) quotes the founder of Reggio: "Teachers must possess a habit of questioning their certainties; a growth of sensitivity, awareness, and availability . . . an enriched evaluation of parental roles; and skills to talk, listen, and learn from parents" (46).

Although roles and approaches of the Learning Community Center differ from those of Reggio Emilia schools in many ways, Anne O'Hara, director of the center, and her staff have meaningful working relationships with families. In the following section, Anne describes a parent and teacher effort to promote and implement a workshop engaging Spanish-speaking families with art and literature.

Engaging Families in Art Play [Anne O'Hara]

One month before the workshop with Hanoch Piven, the staff began creating buzz about the project—talking about Piven and sharing his website with participating families. Isaura, mother of 5-year-old Eduardo, created a one-page flyer to ask families to help us collect materials such as buttons, screws, and hairpins for the workshop. Isaura used the task as an opportunity to practice her English. Families donated items to the center over the course of several weeks, and the center supplemented the materials with more recyclables and art supplies.

More than 115 people showed up for this workshop. Entire families arrived, with children ranging in age from infants to teens. (Children under the age of 3 were cared for by staff in the playroom.) Piven spoke to the crowd in fluent Spanish, putting everyone at ease as he flipped through a slide show of his illustrations and of workshops he had conducted at schools and community centers worldwide. After the presentation, participants headed to a second room for the art workshop.

In the hallway between the two rooms, a long table was covered with the collected materials. Families walked along both sides of this colorful buffet and selected items to use in creating family portraits. Some worked at small tables, and others found space on the hallway floor when the room was full. With a poster board, a cool-melt glue gun, and their collected items, families began their portraits. Piven wove through the room, discussing the emerging creations. Parents and children enjoyed being creative together—using coins for eyes, magnifying glasses for eyeglasses, soft drink tabs for braces, combs for mustaches, and drinking straws for hair. Parents had quality interactions with their children, and children had the rare opportunity to watch their parents become playful and childlike.

Teachers' playful interactions with children promote symbolic play, which is linked to proficiencies in literacy learning.

Considerations

Anne leads a family program that builds on parents' strengths, interests, and needs—key goals for family engagement programming (Weiss, Caspe, & Lopez 2006; Halgunseth et al. 2009). Isaura's handmade flyer, which was copied, distributed, and posted at the center, was pivotal in the success of the project. Because the Learning Community Center's programming includes reciprocity and co-ownership of projects, the flyer moved families to contribute to the collage-materials buffet and to attend the event. An important part of the staff's work is building relationships. A successful family engagement program promotes strengths, emphasizes reciprocity, includes authentic relationships, and builds on the interests and skills of families (Halgunseth et al. 2009).

In the collaborative family workshop environment, the director and staff interacted with families through art play, helped find materials and glue guns, and served as collaborators when asked. The art-play experience offered the staff a relaxed venue for talking with, listening to, and learning from families.

Art Play in the Classroom

Art play as a teaching strategy is contingent on teachers' planning. For the art and play to truly come from the child, teachers prepare environments with materials and an objective for both the art product and goal, guiding children in learning through interactions while children explore, play, and create with art materials. Reed, Hirsh-Pasek, and Golinkoff (2012) advocate strong curricular approaches that are crucial for successful preschool education, and they argue for guided play as an effective approach to meet learning objectives. Weisberg, Hirsh-Pasek, and Golinkoff (2013) define *guided play* as being "midway between direct instruction and free play, presenting a learning goal, and scaffolding the environment while allowing children to maintain a large degree of control over their own learning" (104). Piven-inspired portrait work includes meeting curricular goals through art play. For a collage portrait process to include playfulness with learning, a risk-safe classroom culture is at the foundation while symbolization is at its core.

In the collage portrait, symbolic representation is part of the art process. For young children, symbolic representation happens when a child transforms a birthday candle into an eyebrow while constructing a face. The symbolic representation in the collage technique is part of the creative play scenario—playful exploration of materials, trial and error, and the use of flexible thinking are at work. Using symbolic representation in art play is an important step toward moving children's thinking from the concrete to the symbolic representation of words. In the art process, children move from the concept of a real face (the concrete) to a work of art that symbolizes the real thing (iconic representation). This process lays the groundwork for children to reach higher levels of symbolization—for example, when the word *face* (the symbolic) represents a real face. Art offers children an important experiential bridge, helping them move from the concrete to the symbolic world of words. For preschoolers, the playful collage technique with peer interactions and teacher guidance opens up multiple opportunities for symbolic representation and language development.

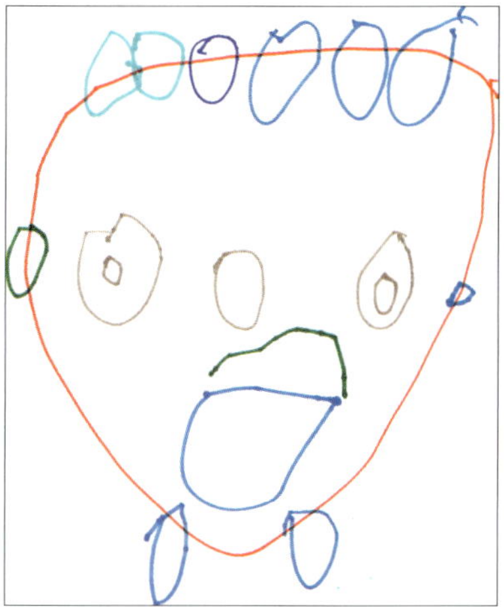

Art is beneficial for all children, including those with special needs. Some may need adaptations to fully participate in art play. For example, children with fine motor needs may find it easier to grasp markers or paintbrushes if a foam curler is placed around them. Children with intellectual disabilities may benefit from fewer materials presented at one time or from additional peer or adult support.

Loretta Novotny teaches a Head Start class in which most children are African American and from families with low incomes. She engaged the children in a study of faces as part of a larger "All About Me" project.

Art Play and Learning [Loretta Novotny]

In a study of faces, the children observed facial features, described their functions, and explored the five senses. To show the concept of symmetry, I cut apart an apple, a kiwi, and a bear-shaped graham cracker to demonstrate that the two halves looked the same. By folding a large photograph of each child's face in half, then opening it up, children discovered symmetry in their faces. They observed where the eyes, nose, ears, and mouth are located on the face.

The children drew their self-portraits during center time. I asked them to describe a make-believe function of the parts on their faces.

Mrs. Novotny: What if a body part, like your hair, could do something else?

Tyrell: Oh, like superpowers?

Mrs. Novotny: Sure.

Tyrell: I want them [my hair] to bump into bad guys.

Mrs. Novotny: What about your nose?

Tyrell: Blow fire out.

Mrs. Novotny: How about you, Karma?

Karma, 3 years old, doesn't catch on, and offers answers that match the function of the facial feature: the nose could get an earring, the mouth could spit out something. She takes a greater risk with hair.

Karma: I want my hair to be like beans, and my bean-hair can talk.

Mrs. Novotny: Well, what would the bean-hair say?

Karma: They'd do something cool—like say I love you.

We also read several children's books. *Let's Make Faces,* by Hanoch Piven, inspired the children to create their own faces using different materials. First, they made faces out of dough. They kneaded the dough and pressed it into the shapes of their faces.

Our recyclable and repurposed objects came from the classroom and the science room, homes, and outdoors. The children placed the objects they collected on a big plastic tray, then they sifted through them, exploring with their hands and describing them. After giving them time to explore, I suggested the children add facial features to their portraits.

Kenesha: *(sifts through the objects)* Ooh, something is spiky.

Tyrell: *(picks up a pencil)* This is a pencil. *(pokes holes in the clay to create hair)*

Andrew: Can I have that for a minute, Tyrell? Can I have that for a minute? *(points to the pencil)*

Tyrell hands Andrew the pencil.

Mrs. Novotny: What are you going to use for your hair?

Karma: Kenesha, I found a barrette. *(hands it to Kenesha)*

Mrs. Novotny: You can use that if you want to, Kenesha.

(Kenesha gives it back to Karma. Karma presses the barrette onto the dough face, then asks Mrs. Novotny to take it out of the dough.)

Mrs. Novotny: Kenesha, what are you going to use for your hair?

Kenesha: I'm going to use . . . *(before finishing the sentence, she picks up wood sticks and places them on the clay face as hair; next, she picks up counting bears)* We have bears? *(and puts the counting bear back down)*

Tyrell: *(sets a sponge on his dough face for hair, then takes it off)* Can you glue this?

Mrs. Novotny: Can you press it into the clay? *(helps Tyrell press the sponge into the clay)*

Considerations

Loretta's teaching strategy included art and guided play as she implemented the class project on faces. She offered the children materials that could spark exploration, interaction, and interest. By posing questions, Loretta led the children from exploration of the materials to achievement of curricular objectives such as developing language and conceptual understanding of facial features and placement. The conversation with 5-year-old Tyrell and 3-year-old Karma allowed Tyrell to create superpowers for his facial features and model the game for Karma. After trying a few (safe) reality-based scenarios, she

Families and Play

Some families may be reluctant to create a space for art exploration at home because they don't have room or are concerned about the mess children might make. They may feel children should be doing "academic" activities or feel they do not know how to support art play. Teachers can create a family art-play tote for children to take home that minimizes mess and enhances creativity. No glue is required for these activities; instead, children use large pieces of felt as backgrounds and repurposed materials to create their art, and when they are done they may either put the materials away or begin another art-play adventure.

Include the following items in the tote to begin with:

- Repurposed materials such as scraps of cloth, lids, plastic netting bags from fruit, discarded silk flowers
- Felt rectangles (known as felt "squares") in various colors to serve as background for the creations
- Yarn and/or ribbons for outlining pictures or creating hair or grass
- A children's book that sparks imagination. Wordless picture books such as *Journey* (2013), by Aaron Becker, engage children and families in imagining and creating the words for pictures; *Red Rubber Boot Day* (2005), by Mary Lyn Ray, offers ideas for pretend play on a rainy day
- A writing journal for families to document the imaginative stories that emerge from art play and send back to the program to share with others

Use these suggestions to talk with families about what children gain from art play and how to encourage art exploration:

- The process of creating art encourages playfulness and stimulates children's imagination. Children who are free to work with art materials might pretend their materials are play objects and engage in fantasy play, or transform their art into something else altogether. Encourage families to write down stories that emerge from their children's art play and read them together.
- Playing together as a family with the items in the art-play tote can enhance children's learning. For example, the features of a dog (and many other animals) are a tail, four legs, two ears, and a head, neck, and body. Creating a dog together or guiding the child to create it while reminding her of the dog's features—if the child is developmentally ready for this—may help her understand the concept of *dog* more fully. Remind families to keep such activities playful and to let children use the materials as they wish.
- Listening to children and responding to them as they play with materials and create stories gives families insight into children's thinking. Discussing children's actions and their creations also supports their vocabulary development and discrimination skills, which are important for reading.
- Just as with play, children sometimes use open-ended art experiences to work through their understanding of and emotions surrounding life events. For example, they might use a box and jar lids to construct a moving van sculpture or collage as they process their concerns over a recent family move.
- Photographing the family art-play tote creations and writing about them in the journal will help children share these exciting experiences with their teachers and peers.

joined in by imagining new functions for her fantasy bean-hair. Teachers' playful interactions with children promote symbolic play, which is linked to proficiencies in literacy learning (Nicolopoulou, McDowell, & Brockmeyer 2006).

While meeting curricular objectives in a playful way, the project allowed children to choose interesting materials that guided their creations. Art play is explorative, constructive, and flexible. Art play that incorporates guided play is similar to the art process described in the Reggio Emilia literature (Malaguzzi & Musatti 1996).

Art Play Introduces the Language of Emotions

Reggio-inspired projects can help young children learn the language of emotions—facial expressions, posture, and voice, for example, communicate how we feel—and we have many emotions to understand and communicate. One hallmark of the Reggio Emilia experience is revisiting concepts under study in multiple ways through many languages (modes of expression—for example, singing, dancing, acting, representing). In the Reggio Emilia project described earlier, children observed themselves using mirrors and photographs, then drew self-portraits. They explored facial expressions and artistically depicted concepts such as "a brain that is happy," "sad hands are closed," and "eyes are shaped like a puddle" (Malaguzzi & Musatti 1996, 50–51). When children explore facial expressions in self-portraits, they are introduced to the vocabulary of emotions such as *happy*, *sad*, and *angry*, and they begin to develop emotional literacy.

Emotional literacy is "the ability to identify, understand, and respond to emotions in oneself and others in a healthy manner" (Joseph, Strain, & Ostrosky 2005, 1). Encouraging children to discuss vocabulary related to emotions allows them to better communicate their feelings and aids in their emotional development because they may be able to understand their emotional experiences.

Theodora Kyle is a prekindergarten teacher whose multi-lingual classroom includes children who are migrants and refugees from Burma, Nepal, and Bhutan. She engaged the class in a study of body parts, and in the process introduced concepts of emotions.

Exploring the Language of Emotions Through Art Play [Theodora Kyle]

Because the class I teach includes children with multiple home languages, a primary goal is to provide a positive, safe, and nurturing environment in which children feel free to explore and investigate. Such environments help children feel comfortable expressing their own physical and emotional issues. Helping children to identify their own body parts and emotions is an

Early Childhood Teacher Candidates' Self Portraits Inspired by Hanoch Piven

In an introduction to the study of creativity in early childhood education, and as a way to introduce themselves to their classmates, teacher candidates at the University of Nebraska Omaha made collage self-portraits using repurposed and found materials. Indicative of Piven's art is the inclusion of objects that symbolize key dimensions of the students' lives.

Emma

I love exploring nature and being outdoors, so I chose to include bark in my hair, grass eyelashes, and a flower for my lips. I chose pennies for my eyes because although my eyes are brown and all of my features are dark, sometimes the light brings out copper flecks. Freckles are represented by coffee beans because my daily life sometimes demands caffeine. My nose is a peace sign because it is in the center of my portrait and in my life I strive for balance through kindness, peace, and being centered.

Sarah

My baby son was born with a congenital heart defect (why my cheeks are hearts). He currently lives in the neonatal intensive care unit at Children's Hospital. Since his birth, I feel all I do is pump (why milk storage bags serve as my hair). It is all I can do to help him at this point. Right now my life is a sterile environment (why the surgical mask serves as my mouth) where my hands are tied (why finger traps serve as my eyebrows). My days and weeks often feel like a yo-yo of emotion—there are many ups and downs. However, my son has many people all around the world praying for him (globe as nose). With their support, I will remember to focus on the positives (smile on the yo-yo face). My son is my life now.

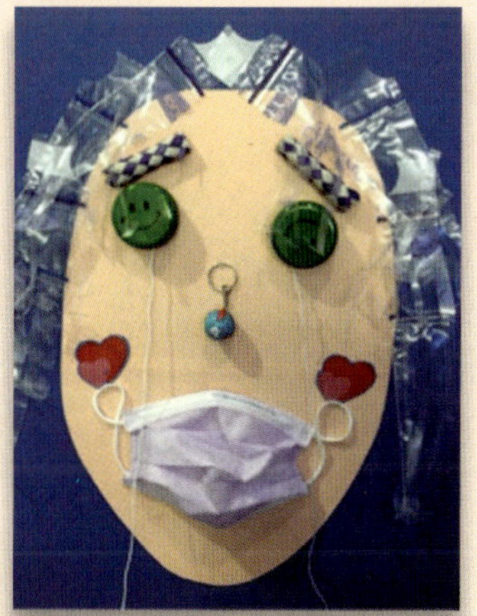

important teaching goal because children can learn to express their feelings in a healthy and positive way. Using picture books to teach vocabulary makes learning more visual, engaging, and meaningful.

I found Piven's *Let's Make Faces* very useful for our study of body parts. Through this book, children learned to identify the eyes, nose, mouth, ears, and hair in English. As children learned about the parts of the face, they saw that faces express feelings, which served as an introduction to the vocabulary of emotions. We focused on happy, sad, and angry emotions by reading books about feelings and having discussions prompted by my questions, such as "How do you know when your friend is sad?" and "What can you do to help her out?"

Memo to: All Families of Young Children
From: Diane E. Levin
Date: January 2015
Subject: **Advocating for Play at School and at Home**

Play is essential for children's optimal development and learning. Through play children use what they already know to help them figure out new things, see how they work, and master skills. As they do this, children add new social, emotional, and intellectual knowledge and skills to what they already know. They experience the satisfaction that comes from working things out and solving problems on their own. They think and sometimes say out loud, "I can do it!" This is the kind of learning through play that prepares children to feel confident in themselves as learners who see new information and ideas as interesting problems to be solved.

However, all play is not the same, and today several forces can endanger quality play. First, the use of fast-paced and push-button electronic media takes young children away from play and can make their slower-paced child-created play seem boring. Second, many of today's toys are linked to what children see in movies and on television and channel children into imitating what they see on screens instead of creating their own play and engaging in problem solving. Finally, growing pressure to teach academic skills at younger and younger ages takes time and resources away from the quality, teacher-facilitated play that young children need in preschool and kindergarten.

I encourage you to learn about the ways child-created active play supports learning and to advocate for play and encourage it at home. Play will give your children a foundation for positive social and emotional health as well as later academic success in school.

Diane E. Levin, PhD, is a professor of early childhood education at Wheelock College, in Boston. She is a cofounder of Teachers Resisting Unhealthy Children's Entertainment (www.truceteachers.org) and Defending the Early Years (www.deyproject.org).

I concluded the study of the parts of the face and the introduction to the concept that faces show emotions with the portrait collage project inspired by *Let's Make Faces*. The collage workshop allowed children who are dual language learners to use their knowledge and vocabulary for parts of the face and emotions in a nonthreatening and creative manner.

I began by scattering collage materials for the project on a table and allowing the children the time they needed to explore and play with them. Examining the materials ahead of time sparked their curiosity and interest, prompted dialogue with peers, and allowed them time to think about what pieces they might use to create their own self-portraits.

As the children created their portraits, I encouraged the use of emotions vocabulary by suggesting they make a happy face, a sad face, or an angry face. To my surprise, only one child out of 16 drew a representation of an emotion on her portrait. This may have been a result of the children's limited understanding of English vocabulary or of their focus on making sure they included all the parts of the face in their portraits.

Later, many of the children drew faces during choice time, either in the writing center or in the art center. Anna brought her picture to me and pointed to a mouth. I said, "Oh, I see you made a face. I see two eyes and a mouth." Then I asked, "Is she happy or sad?" Anna replied, "Sad." I asked, "Why is she sad?" She said, "Because her mom is gone." Anna was able to answer my question, which meant that she understood the emotional concept of sad.

Considerations

Theodora's story illustrates how playful exploration with art and creating faces helps teachers introduce vocabulary about emotions, an important aspect of promoting emotional literacy in young children. Exploring emotions through art can also be very beneficial for children who struggle to express their emotions in healthy ways.

Although her experience may show that the children had a very basic understanding of emotions, Theodora viewed this as a starting point—it was where the children were at the moment. She was excited to see that the children had begun to notice emotions in stories and were identifying them using the vocabulary they had learned. By engaging the children in art play and introducing the language of emotions, Theodora sparked their development of emotional literacy.

Conclusion

The authors began a school- and community-based literacy project that brought an author/illustrator of children's books to conduct collage portrait workshops. The big difference between this project and our past OFLP projects was the presence of art play in the workshop. Embedded in this project across the sites were exploration, symbolism, interaction, and engagement. Participants interacted and responded to collage materials, causing language and literacy development to flow in all three settings and making for a richer experience than in past OFLP author/illustrator projects, which predominantly centered on guest speakers' presentations.

Experiencing the collage process in a family event and also in pre-K through grade 6 classrooms helps children and adults understand the illustrator's process. It made the OFLP planning group think differently about how to implement future family book celebrations with authors and illustrators. The workshop encouraged a playful spirit as families created self-portraits. Through art play, teachers can intentionally guide learning and introduce vocabulary using activities related to children's books.

> I understood that it wasn't really about creating art. It was about telling stories. It was about communicating. Playfulness through the use of collage was allowing people to tell a story through art which perhaps would have been too difficult to say in words.
>
> —*Hanoch Piven,* "Living in a Playful Collage"

References

Ahn, J., & M. Filipenko. 2007. "Narrative, Imaginary Play, Art, and Self: Intersecting Worlds." *Early Childhood Education Journal* 34 (4): 279–89.

Anning, A., & K. Ring. 2004. *Making Sense of Children's Drawings.* Maidenhead, UK: Open University Press.

Bentley, D.F. 2013. *Everyday Artists: Inquiry and Creativity in the Early Childhood Classroom.* New York: Teachers College Press.

Bhroin, M.N. 2007. "'A Slice of Life': The Interrelationships Among Art, Play, and the 'Real' Life of the Young Child." *International Journal of Education and the Arts* 8 (16): 1–25. www.ijea.org/v8n16.

Gandini, L. 2012. "History, Ideas, and Basic Principles: An Interview With Loris Malaguzzi." Chap. 2 in *The Hundred Languages of Children: The Reggio Emilia Experience in Transformation,* 3rd ed., eds. C. Edwards, L. Gandini, & G. Forman, 27–72. Santa Barbara, CA: Praeger.

Halgunseth, L.C., A. Peterson, D.R. Stark, & S. Moodie. 2009. "Family Engagement, Diverse Families, and Early Childhood Education Programs: An Integrated Review of the Literature." Washington, DC: NAEYC & Pre-K Now. www.naeyc.org/files/naeyc/file/research/FamEngage.pdf.

Joseph, G., P. Strain, & M.M. Ostrosky. 2005. *Fostering Emotional Literacy in Young Children: Labeling Emotions.* What Works Brief 21. Center on the Social and Emotional Foundations for Early Learning. http://csefel.vanderbilt.edu/briefs/wwb21.pdf.

Kolbe, U. 2005a. *It's Not a Bird Yet: The Drama of Drawing.* Byron Bay, NSW, Australia: Peppinot.

Kolbe, U. 2005b. *Rapunzel's Supermarket: All About Young Children and Their Art.* 2nd ed. Byron Bay, NSW, Australia: Peppinot.

Malaguzzi, L., & C. Musatti. 1996. "L 'Importanza di Rivedersi / The Importance of Seeing Yourself Again." In *I cento linguaggi dei bambini: Narrativa del possibile/The Hundred Languages of Children: Narrative of the Possible,* eds. T. Filippini & V. Vecchi, 46–52. Reggio Emilia, Italy: Reggio Children.

Nicolopoulou, A., J. McDowell, & C. Brockmeyer. 2006. "Narrative Play and Emergent Literacy: Storytelling and Story-Acting Meet Journal Writing." Chap. 7 in *Play = Learning: How Play Motivates and Enhances Children's Cognitive and Social-Emotional Growth,* eds. D.G. Singer, R.M. Golinkoff, & K. Hirsh-Pasek, 124–44. New York: Oxford University Press.

Ostroff, W.L. 2012. *Understanding How Young Children Learn: Bringing the Science of Child Development to the Classroom.* Alexandria, VA: ASCD.

Reed, J., K. Hirsh-Pasek, & R.M. Golinkoff. 2012. "A Tale of Two Schools: The Promise of Playful Learning." Chap. 2 in *Defending Childhood: Keeping the Promise of Early Education,* ed. B. Falk, 24–47. New York: Teachers College Press.

Weisberg, D.S., K. Hirsh-Pasek, & R.M. Golinkoff. 2013. "Guided Play: Where Curricular Goals Meet a Playful Pedagogy." *Mind, Brain, and Education* 7 (2): 104–12.

Weiss, H.B., M. Caspe, & M.E. Lopez. 2006. "Family Involvement in Early Childhood Education." *Family Involvement Makes a Difference* 1 (Spring): 1–8. www.hfrp.org/publications-resources/browse-our-publications/family-involvement-in-early-childhood-education.

Lisa D. Wood

Holding on to Play: Reflecting on Experiences as a Playful K–3 Teacher

Play and learning through play form the foundation of who I am as an early childhood professional. It has been my joy and honor to work and play with children, families, teachers, and communities throughout my career. My own childhood was full of play; it is a part of me, a part of my life story that I happily carry with me to this day.

Play is important for brain, cognitive, linguistic, physical, psychological, and social-emotional development and well-being. It is also a vitally important basic human need, with transformative potential (Sutton-Smith 1997; Brown & Vaughan 2009). For these reasons, the intersection of play and developmentally appropriate practice has guided my philosophy as both learner and teacher—first as a preschool teacher, then as a teacher in public school K–3 classrooms, and now as an instructor of undergraduate students studying early childhood education. I have spent the past few years enthusiastically exploring play, the theory and research behind it, and its relationship to curriculum and practice. What did I learn?

Well, much like Robert Fulghum (2003), I discovered that perhaps all I really need to know I learned in kindergarten! I learned that for my personal well-being, I need to include play in my life, and I need to "play nice" with others

naeyc® 2, 3

(even when other players do not). I learned that I need to make learning visible through documentation, much like show-and-tell, and find my voice as a play advocate through reflective journaling and professional development. I learned from the children I taught that when I allowed time in the classroom for play and trusted its vital importance, children learned, thrived, and grew by leaps and bounds! And finally, I learned that "no man is an island," and that all players need a village.

Children need advocates for play, while teachers need a village to support their role as play-based early childhood education advocates.

Gather Your Village

When I reflect on my successes and challenges in implementing play-based curricula, especially in public school settings, I remember that one of my key approaches was keeping an open door. I often left the classroom door open as an invitation to families and other community members to come in, see what we were exploring, and play and learn *with* us. My hope was to create communal bonds across grade levels throughout the school, and to increase understanding of the value of a play-based curriculum among families and other teachers. However, that left me, a novice teacher, personally open to scrutiny and judgment, some of which I wasn't ready for. Consider this selection taken from one of my early kindergarten journal reflections, demonstrating my joys and self-doubts:

> Bursts of sunlight stream through the windows of my kindergarten classroom and cast an array of prisms across the room. It is as if the sun illuminates our play invitations and entices players to explore the special items offered for their use. I am prepared to circulate around the room with my camera in my apron pocket and my clipboard in hand. I am eager to document observations and take dictation. As I scan the room I see children deeply engaged in the flow of play and learning. At the science center a pair of children busily explores spectrums and prisms, while another pair investigates rainbows with watercolor-filled beakers and eyedroppers. An adjacent trio intently explores the unexpected physical properties of a concoction of gluey gloop. The children are smiling, laughing, and talking about the surprise of their discoveries. . . .
>
> Enya's song "Only Time" billows softly through the air until the flow of our play, or my enjoyment of it, is interrupted by my nagging doubts—what I've come to think of as my classroom bully—formed by negative thoughts, vulnerability, and questions that start to bubble up. "Exactly how will this benefit children's future test scores? How do I explain that they are learning and I am teaching, when it looks like we're all having so much fun? How can I justify including an outdoor recess later?"

As a novice teacher, I was full of commitment to, and faith in, play as the core of my curriculum. However, I did not have the words or the confidence to explain the magic of what was happening—the connection of children's playful experiences with their construction of knowledge and development of critical skills.

When I look back on that journal entry, I see clearly that the children were immersed in what Csikszentmihalyi calls *flow*: "Flow is the way people describe their state of mind when consciousness is harmoniously ordered, and they want to pursue whatever they are doing for its own sake" (1990, 6). I now have the language and the confidence to describe what I was doing and why it was important, but I have all-too-painful memories of redness creeping across my face and of bumbling through explanations of why play is important and how my teaching practices were helping children learn. I am not sure how convincing I was in my first years of public school teaching. I often felt my values shaken to the core: I needed more knowledge and language to advocate for play, and I needed to

Lisa D. Wood, MS, is a curriculum writer, associate instructor, and doctoral candidate in the Curriculum and Instruction, Early Childhood and Art Education program at Indiana University, in Bloomington. Lisa has worked as a pre-K–3 educator in public and private settings, and now teaches preservice educators. Her research focuses on play, well-being, supporting teachers, the Reggio Emilia experience, creativity, and qualitative and arts-based research methods.

work harder to document play to make learning visible. And I knew I would need to gather a village to help keep play alive and keep at bay the bullies from inside my head and outside the classroom door.

In *It Takes a Village,* Hillary Rodham Clinton reminds us about our need for a village: "The village can no longer be defined as a place on a map, or a list of people or organizations, but its essence remains the same: it is the network of values and relationships that support and affect our lives" (1996, 9). As we continue to see movement away from play and play-based learning in primary settings, now more than ever children and teachers need a village. Children need advocates for play, while teachers need a village to support their role as play-based early childhood education advocates. Moreover, teachers need the support of a village to empower and nurture their ongoing efforts to provide developmentally appropriate play experiences.

In Vivian Gussin Paley's keynote address at the 2011 NAEYC Annual Conference and Expo, she called on attendees to consider, "Who will save the kindergarten?" With the push down of academic expectations in primary grades, kindergarten, and preschool, the answer to this question likely depends on gathering a broader group of play advocates, including parents, preschool through grade 12 teachers and administrators, community members, foundations, museums, higher education faculty, and policy makers.

Tug-of-War: Hold on Tight!

In the elementary setting in particular, remaining wholly committed to developmentally appropriate play-based curricula can be challenging. NAEYC guidelines for developmentally appropriate practice recommend that teachers provide "experiences, materials, and interactions to enable children to engage in play that allows them to stretch their boundaries to the fullest in their imagination, language, interaction, and self-regulation" (2009, 18).

Like a game of tug-of-war, some teachers feel torn between honoring their philosophical grounding in developmentally appropriate practice and play and meeting mandates, closing the learning gap, and demonstrating accountability to administrators and the public at large. A K–3 teacher recently told me, "With high accountability, countless demands, and mandates, I simply feel defeated, burned out. And after all these years of teaching, I am even beginning to question my beliefs about play! How can this be happening? What can I do?" We must remain firm in holding on to play as important in our guiding philosophies, holding fast to the promise to provide opportunities for play. Here are some strategies:

- Gather your village
  - Seek out supportive mentors, colleagues, and administrators
  - Include and involve parents, families, and community members
  - Reach out to organizations, museums, foundations, and institutions
  - Create communal bonds; hold advocacy events
- Build your play language and find your voice
  - Become well versed in developmentally appropriate practice
  - Keep knowledge current by reading articles, books, and research
  - Build play language for advocacy with professional development
- Make benefits of play visible
  - Use documentation, dictation, exhibition, and events to make the benefits of play in your classroom visible to the outside world
- Keep a journal
  - Use reflective journaling to empower yourself and your practice

Truth is, holding on to a commitment to be a play-based teacher is even more difficult now than when I was a classroom teacher. It seems to get tougher with each passing year. Current trends toward standardized curriculum and test-based content have led to an increase in time for direct instruction and a decrease in time for children to play in kindergarten. Between 1998 and 2011, there has been a significant decrease in the inclusion of hands-on math/science manipulatives, puzzles, blocks, art, dramatic play, and sand/water table play in the kindergarten classroom (Walston 2013). "Kindergartners today are facing: More focus on rigorous academic skills, less focus on music, art, and creative activities, and higher academic and behavioral expectations when they enter kindergarten" (34). This might explain why novice and veteran kindergarten teachers alike feel they can no longer hold fast in their promise to play in kindergarten.

Play *Is* What It's All About!

It is an exciting time for play, and teachers should feel hopeful. As I continue to reflect on my experiences and what I have learned from research about play and children's learning, I am more convinced now than ever that play *is* what it's all about! In fact, play has become the focus of much serious research over the past several years. "Playfulness (the drive to play) serves educative purposes complementary to those of curiosity. While curiosity motivates children to seek new knowledge and understanding, playfulness motivates them to practice new skills and use those skills creatively" (Gray 2013, 118). Scholars are speaking out on behalf of play and its benefits. Consider the words of researcher and theorist Stuart Brown:

> We are built to play and built through play. When we play, we are engaged in the purest expression of our humanity, the truest expression of our individuality. Is it any wonder that often the times we feel most alive, those that make up our best memories, are moments of play? (Brown & Vaughan 2009, 5)

Drawing from neuroscience and cognitive, social, and developmental research, Brown invites a broad awareness of the importance of play and its vital role in well-being: "Play isn't the enemy of learning, it's learning's partner. Play is like fertilizer for brain growth. It's crazy not to use it" (Brown & Vaughan 2009, 101). Brown further emphasizes that play helps us reach our maximum developmental and neurological potential by contributing positively to our physical, emotional, psychological, and social development.

Play contributes to the development of creativity, optimism, and innovation. Pretend play offers children the opportunity to express "many different processes—cognitive, affective, and interpersonal—important for creativity" (Russ & Wallace 2013, 136), and theorists and researchers conclude that "pretend play and creativity are linked" (136). Pretend play allows children to creatively and symbolically play with objects, use their imaginations, and tell stories (Russ & Wallace 2013). It allows children to experiment with role-playing and narrative to imagine how they might navigate through their ever-changing world: "Children bring the realities of their world into a fictional context, where it is safe to confront them, to experience them, and to practice ways of dealing

Are the Benefits of Play Visible in Your Classroom?

This checklist suggests ways to show the role of play in the learning process and advocate for play in your classroom.

- ❑ Document and take dictation regularly throughout the day
- ❑ Display child-created work prominently in the classroom and in the hall
- ❑ Display prominently digital images of children playing, working, exploring, creating, and making indoors and outdoors in my classroom and in the hall
- ❑ Pair visual displays of images and children's work with documentation
- ❑ Display documentation of brainstorming activities, children's emergent dictation, and dialogue to provide a road map of the thinking/learning process
- ❑ Involve parents, children, and community members in documentation

Include the following in your documentation:

- ❑ Research, curriculum, pedagogical, theoretical, or inspirational quotes to support play, developmentally appropriate practice, physical, social, and emotional growth
- ❑ Standards, core curriculum, early childhood foundations, developmental milestones, and teaching proficiencies that apply
- ❑ Descriptions of properties of play, play personalities, and play processes

Families and Play

These tips suggest ways to build play partnerships with families and communicate the importance of play throughout the year.

Back to School

- Build the foundation for a play partnership by hosting a back-to-school play event. Here are some suggestions:
    - Introduce families to play and playful learning in their children's learning environment with a visual presentation. Explain why play is important and the ways you observe, document, and/or assess the learning and development children gain through play. Follow with an interactive discussion about nurturing your play partnership.
    - Invite administrators, principals, and staff to attend the event, play, and explain their role in supporting children, families, and play.
    - Use the suggestions inspired by play personalities (see p. 94) to engage both adults and children in play. Join in and share your playful nature!
    - Invite family members to draw and/or write about their favorite play memories and children to draw and/or write about their own play interests. Encourage them to display their creations side by side on a documentation wall.
    - Encourage families to ask questions and share feedback about play and participating in a play partnership.
    - Cocreate written promises or commitments to play and playful learning.
    - Provide time for children and families to play actively outdoors or in a gross motor room.
    - Conclude by gathering families for a playful communal activity.
    - Invite everyone to cheer a promise to support the cocreated commitment!

Daily

- Make the benefits of play visible through documentation (see the checklist on p. 91).
- Share playful images and documentation narratives on your classroom website or blog.
- Welcome families' questions and concerns by exchanging dialogue or anecdotal notes about their children's play at school and home, their interests, and their friendships.
- Build a family lending library that includes resources about the importance of play, along with play materials such as games, cards, puppets, and toys.

Weekly

- Feature mini-documentation panels and family-friendly quotes, research, and resources about the importance of play in your newsletter.
- Highlight one family each week by sharing stories and images of their family at play.
- Inform families of playful opportunities, resources, and community events.
- Engage families in an interactive Q&A forum about play or playful learning, or provide a question box. Respond with current information, and provide examples from children's learning environment or at home.

Monthly/Bi-Monthly

- Engage in individual and group discussions with families about play and its importance.
- Encourage families to form, join, and participate in organizational play advocacy groups or events in the community.
- Collaborate with families to plan monthly/bimonthly play events.
- Host a family play night. Share a short skit, video, or slideshow about the importance of play to kick off the night's events, and invite families to share their own traditional or cultural play activities.

100th Day of School

- Partner with families to organize a "100 Days/Ways of Play and Playful Learning" celebration.

School Year Grand Finale

- Reflect and share stories, images, and dialogue with families to celebrate a playful year of growth, learning, and well-being.
- Share ideas and opportunities for extending play and playful learning over the summer break.
- PLAY!

with them" (Gray 2013, 169). These kinds of play experiences scaffold the creativity, imagination, optimism, coping, resilience, and social-emotional development essential to well-being. David Elkind further emphasizes that play is a part of our creative drive, as a fundamental mode of learning and a "basic right of childhood!" (2007, xvii). Richard Louv is leading the movement to bring pretend play and all kinds of play outdoors, and to save children from what he calls "nature deficit disorder" (2008, 10).

For teachers, an important step is to find or rediscover our voice and our ability to express the importance of play and developmentally appropriate practice. Understanding the properties, personalities, processes, stages, and states of play (Brown & Vaughan 2009), as I teach them now to preservice teachers, helps prepare both novice and veteran teachers to embed this knowledge into developmentally appropriate teaching philosophies, curricula, documentation, and classroom environments.

The Beauty of Play

To Stuart Brown, play is "a thing of beauty," and he sees it as critical for animals, children, and adults alike (Brown & Vaughan 2009). He does not, however, give any single, absolute definition of play. Instead, he breaks play into properties that explain the reasons we play and the styles or personalities of play that describe the ways individuals engage in it (see "Brown's Properties of Play" and "Practical Suggestions for K–3 Settings Based on Play Personalities," p. 94). Thinking about play through these frameworks helps teachers to understand, document, and meet the individual needs of children through the classroom environment—creating the right setup and design, selecting materials, and varying instruction and facilitation to scaffold learning. These play frameworks give us yet another lens through which to observe and document children's growth and learning through the "beauty of play," and to reflect on our practice to better support the individual needs of all children.

Brown's Properties of Play

Stuart Brown breaks play into seven properties that explain the reasons we play and the styles or personalities of play that describe the ways individuals engage in it.

- **Apparently purposeless:** No obvious survival value; play for play's sake
- **Voluntary:** Not required; optional
- **Inherent attraction:** Exciting, attractive, feels good
- **Freedom from time:** Lose sense of time
- **Diminished consciousness of self:** Lose self in the zone or flow of play; during imaginative play, might pretend to be a different self
- **Improvisation potential:** Lose rigidity in the way we do things; open to chance, opportunity, and serendipity
- **Continuation desire:** A drive or desire to keep doing it

Adapted with permission from Brown & Vaughan (2009), 17–18.

Empowering Your Practice Through Creative/Reflective Journaling

These tips will help you make journaling a part of your routine to empower your inner player and nurture yourself as a teacher.

- Record observations and reflect on the classroom environment, invitations, dialogue, daily life, and play.
- Reflect on your celebrations, struggles, and hopes.
- Brainstorm child-centered interests and needs as they emerge.
- Record ideas for emergent curricula and play invitations to entice children to explore special activities and materials.
- Create webs and mind maps of possible integration of play within the curriculum.
- Include books, quotes, websites, blogs, and resources to inspire you.
- Reflect on memorable moments as a teacher that remind you of why you teach.
- Write or sketch memories of your own play as a child; discover and embrace your own play personality and inner player.
- Use technology to journal by starting a play blog.
- Play and correspond with your imaginary mentor, someone who inspires you.
- Write questions to ask your imaginary mentor.
- Doodle, sketch, collage, draw, paint, and create comics of yourself and the classroom.
- Create a cover for your journal, or allow time for your cover to emerge and evolve.

Practical Suggestions for K–3 Settings Based on Play Personalities

Personality	Teaching Strategies	What Children Learn
The Joker enjoys nonsense, baby talk, practical jokes, pranks, horseplay, and comedy	Provide lighthearted opportunities for comedy, joke telling/writing. Include: children's joke books, riddles, poetry, prose, toy microphones, stage props, silly hats, costumes for play and improvisation.	**Language Development:** Increased vocabulary, speaking audibly, expressing thoughts, feelings, and ideas clearly. Speaking and listening during interactive conversations. Anticipation of tones, cues, phrases, facial expressions, and conversational reciprocation.
The Kinesthete loves to move, dance, walk, swim, and participate in sports (movement is the focus, not competition)	Integrate body movement into indoor/outdoor curriculum, activities, and lessons. Include yoga, dance, and stretching during transitions. Enjoy indoor/outdoor movement activities with the children!	**Gross Motor Development:** Strength, balance, and stability through movement and control of body parts, repetition/imitation of actions via direct instruction or improvisation; rhythm and free-form movement. **Math Concepts:** While moving, count to 100 by ones, fives, and tens. **Social-Emotional Development:** Well-being, body movement/emotion.
The Explorer engages in physical, emotional, mental, and creative exploration of our world and imaginations	Provide opportunities for inquiry, indoor and outdoor exploration, creativity, problem solving, sand/water and other sensory experiences. Include natural and found objects, field guides, binoculars, magnifying glasses, containers for exploring/collecting samples or artifacts, maps, mapmaking invitations, multicultural dolls/figures, cooking utensils, dress-up clothes, and props.	**Science, Math, Geography, Social Studies, Literacy Concepts:** Scientific method, inquiry, experimentation, sorting, identification, measurement, similarities, differences, physical properties and attributes of artifacts, classification, student-generated writing and drawing activities to describe/document discoveries about the world and living environment around them. **Social Skills:** Self-confidence, discussion, communication, sharing, and collaboration with peers.
The Competitor tends to be less interested in creative engagement, enjoys playing rule-bound games and winning	Provide indoor/outdoor curricular and free play opportunities for physical game playing, board games, and other forms of games.	**Math Concepts:** Problem solving, counting, sequencing, pairing and shapes recognition. **Physical Development:** Fine/gross motor. Social-**Emotional Development:** Following simple rules, cooperation, turn taking. **Literacy Concepts:** Reading or listening to instructions.
The Director loves power and is a born organizer	Provide child-directed open materials and invitations: blocks, puzzles, object sorting, letters, counting, mapmaking, organization, and time for free play. Try setting up a recycling center for classification and sorting.	**Social-Emotional Development:** Invitations, open materials to foster social-emotional development, autonomy, and confidence. **Math, Science, and Literacy Concepts:** Sorting, counting, classification, organization, direction, and sequence of events.

(continued)

Personality	Teaching Strategies	What Children Learn
The Collector is interested in collecting objects or experiences	Provide opportunities to collect objects and natural materials; allow children time to collage, document, and share objects, interests, and experiences.	**Math, Social Studies, Art, Geography, Science, Literacy Concepts:** Artifact telling, retelling, and storytelling in oral, written, and visual form. Sorting and expressing preferences for object attributes and collage design.
The Artist/Creator enjoys making, creating artwork, tinkering, and inventing	Provide a variety of open-ended artistic materials and open time for art making, sensory experiences, cartooning, tinkering, creating, and inventing. Provide a wide range of recycled and natural materials, cardboard boxes, clock or machine parts, and tinkering tools to inspire imagination and invention.	**Art, Creativity, Fine Motor Development, Sustainability:** Understanding physical properties/manipulation of art materials; visual representation, color properties/recognition, use of line, repetition, texture, shape, emotion, planning, abstract vs. realism; self-expression, sensory experience, meaning making, imagination, invention, problem solving; use of natural/recycled materials.
The Storyteller can be a writer, reader, performer, magician, filmmaker; someone who loves improv and enjoys including themselves in the imaginative stories they tell	Offer a rich array of materials for an ever-changing dramatic play area, including stage, props, costumes, puppets for theater/dramatic play; fairy tales, literature, and time for oral storytelling/story writing. Document student-dictated stories and/or allow students to record themselves with digital recorders or cameras.	**Reading, Language Arts, Language Development, and Technology Concepts:** Reading/love of literature; oral storytelling, acting, and reenacting stories/events; creating, writing, and illustrating stories; describing familiar and imaginary people, places, things, and events; adding details, expressing feelings, thoughts, and ideas associated with stories; documenting stories with technology.

Column one adapted with permission from Brown & Vaughan (2009), 65–70.

Pacify the Bullies

Having experienced my own bullies, I began to read everything I could about documentation, the Reggio Emilia experience, and play. I reached out to mentors, NAEYC members, and supportive colleagues and administrators, and I even visited the schools in Reggio Emilia, Italy, to learn firsthand. And I read, read, and read. Along with reading, I continued to reflect in my journal. I gained particular inspiration from favorite authors and play advocates, including Vivian Gussin Paley. Finding my own inner player, I addressed Vivian Paley in my journals, thinking of her as my imaginary mentor.

Soon I saw my identity expand from teacher to teacher–researcher and advocate. My experiences nurtured and validated my thinking about the role of play and learning in the lives of children. This new understanding prepared me to talk about and defend the importance of play more clearly. For instance, in the classroom and outside the door I posted documentation panels displaying children's emergent narratives and photographs of the children playing—creating, smiling, working, learning, and growing. Alongside these panels I added quotations from authors, psychologists, and theorists explaining the cognitive, linguistic, and social-emotional value, the learning outcomes, and the importance of play and play-based learning. I incorporated smaller versions in family newsletters. I also engaged in individual and group conversations with families about

Olga S. Jarrett,
John Sutterby,
Darlene DeMarie,
and Vera
Stenhouse

Play for All Children: Access to Quality Play Experiences as a Social Justice Issue

We believe, as do developmental theorists (Piaget 1976; Vygotsky 1980), play therapists (Kestly 2014), and researchers (Brown 2010; Gray 2013) that play is essential for children's cognitive, physical, creative, and social-emotional development. In addition, we recognize that the provision of quality play spaces can be a way to ensure that all children have opportunities to play. However, access to quality play spaces in the United States is impacted by disparities related to race, class, and gender. Children's access to play has been limited in three major ways, especially for children whose families have low incomes. Research, including our own (see Jarrett 2013), shows that compared with children who attend schools and live in neighborhoods with greater resources, children in poverty and children from racially underrepresented groups have 1) lower-quality school playgrounds, 2) less time in the daily classroom schedule for recess, and 3) more structured instruction and less playful learning in school from an early age. These patterns of inequity are detrimental to the healthy growth and development of many children.

School Playground Disparities

One visible area of injustice is access to quality play environments. Spending a lot of money on play settings is not, of course, a guarantee that healthy and productive play will occur. Children might play more with a cardboard box than with the toy that came in the box, and natural elements like rocks and sticks and leaves are just as valuable as play materials as purchased items. On the other hand, financial resources can improve play spaces for children when they are used to make an unsafe playground safer or to make an inaccessible playground accessible. If we value democracy in society, we need robust advocacy for inviting public spaces for all children.

To determine whether economic disparities are reflected in school play facilities, Olga and her graduate students at Georgia State University conducted research on all the elementary school playgrounds in one Southern county school system. They took representative photographs of the play equipment, school gardens/nature trails, playing fields, and outdoor art and created pages of photos from each school. Each set of school photos was then scored for quality and quantity of facilities by graduate student raters and analyzed statistically. There were no significant demographic differences in school gardens, the existence of playing fields, or evidence of outdoor art. The gardens and artwork are features that likely reflect the dedication of the teachers. The playing fields were provided by the county. However, the schools in less advantaged neighborhoods had county-issued unimaginative play structures appropriate for only the youngest children, whereas the school communities in wealthier areas had raised money to build more exciting and challenging play structures. (The photo on this page shows typical playground structures from one school system. Note the large drop from the bottom of the slide on the structure in the foreground, which is designed for younger children. Older children have only the blue fitness structure in the background to play on.) Although fancy playgrounds are not necessary for good play, the quality of a playground is likely reflective of the value the school system places on play. (See the contrasting photos from different districts on p. 101.)

Who Gets to Have Recess?

Playground quality is of little importance if children do not have recess. Here also are issues of fairness. In the late 1980s and early 1990s, three of the six school systems in the Atlanta area abolished recess. Teachers were *not allowed* to take children out for recess despite the existence of playgrounds. A study of the demographics of the area school systems with and without recess revealed an obvious pattern. In the three school systems with recess, 21 to 32 percent of the students received free/reduced price lunch (based on family income), and 18 to 39 percent of the student body were Black. In contrast, in

Olga S. Jarrett, PhD, is professor of science education in the Department of Early Childhood Education at Georgia State University.

John Sutterby, PhD, is associate professor in the Department of Interdisciplinary Learning and Teaching at the University of Texas at San Antonio with a research specialty in outdoor play.

Darlene DeMarie, PhD, is associate professor of educational psychology and Fulbright Faculty Advisor at the University of South Florida.

Vera Stenhouse, PhD, is a researcher and consultant with a focus on diversity and multicultural education.

Families and Play

Families want the best for their children, and sometimes they have concerns about their children playing outdoors. Here are some common concerns and ways teachers might address them.

- **I want my child to be ready for school and not just play.**

Children learn in all types of environments. The outdoor play area is their classroom just as the indoor space is. Outdoors, children learn about nature and science. They observe how the trees, flowers, and grass change according to the seasons; they experiment with light and shadows; they notice differences in the sky, wind, and temperature as the weather changes. They take on physical challenges and develop strong bodies as they climb, swing, slide, jump, throw, and ride. As they play together, children learn social skills such as being fair and taking turns. All of these skills prepare children to succeed in school.

- **Children play too rough outside; they might get hurt.**

Children need to be physically active. When they play outside, they learn how to use their bodies in ways that will help them the rest of their life. Children who are more fit and who have learned how to properly move their bodies during active play are less likely to be injured during play (US Department of Health and Human Services 2008).

- **It's too cold (or hot) to play outside. I do not want my child to get sick.**

With appropriate clothing, plus shade, water, and sunscreen, children can be very comfortable outdoors. They will actually be healthier, too: Contact with the diverse organisms in nature helps children's immune systems develop more robustly (see National Wildlife Federation 2012). For most children, more exposure is better for their health and well-being.

- **My child's clothes will get dirty.**

We want children to be active learners, and that means that sometimes they will get dirty. Consider dressing your child in washable clothing that will be okay if stained or send an extra pair of clothes for your child to change into.

References

National Wildlife Federation. 2012. ***The Dirt on Dirt: How Getting Dirty Outdoors Benefits Kids.*** http://www.nwf.org/pdf/Be%20Out%20There/Dirt_Report_2012.pdf.

US Department of Health and Human Services. 2008. ***Physical Activity Guidelines for Americans.*** www.health.gov/paguidelines/pdf/paguide.pdf.

the three Atlanta school systems that did not permit recess, 56 to 80 percent of students received free/reduced price lunch and 68 to 89 percent were Black (Jarrett 2003).

National research conducted with a random sample of children found a similar pattern (Roth et al. 2002). The researchers asked each teacher of a target child to record everything the child did during a randomly selected day. The results showed that only 79 percent of the children in the sample had recess that day; 21 percent did not have recess. The demographic breakdown of who did and did not have recess is even more disturbing. Thirty-nine percent of the Black children did not have recess compared with 15 percent of the White children. Also, 44 percent of the children from families below the poverty line did not have recess; 17 percent of the children from families above the poverty line did not have recess.

Some things have improved over the years in the Atlanta area. All the school systems now allow recess, although some school principals do not encourage it. But surveys of teachers in schools in high-poverty areas show that many children still do not have recess. Two hundred eleven teacher interns and new teachers (162 in pre-K–3) in two university master's programs preparing teachers for high-poverty schools completed anonymous surveys on their recess beliefs and school policies. The survey data, collected in four waves from 2012 to 2014, revealed whether the teachers and interns had provided recess the day of the survey and whether the adults had deprived any children of recess as a form of discipline. With each wave reported separately, results showed that 43 to 78 percent of the classrooms represented had recess the day of the survey. In approximately half of those classrooms with recess, the teacher deprived *some* children of recess as discipline. The percentage of classrooms in which *all* the children had recess ranged from 21 to 52 percent. Boys, specifically Black boys, were most often deprived of recess for infractions, including showing defiance, not finishing their class work, and not bringing a signed note from home.

According to the Centers for Disease Control and Prevention (2010), eight studies of the effects of recess on academic performance or on-task behavior all found beneficial effects. An American Academy of Pediatrics (2013, 183) policy statement asserts that recess is a "crucial and necessary component of a child's development . . . that should not be withheld for punitive or academic reasons." What happens when children don't have recess? Research indicates that children are more fidgety and less on-task when deprived of recess (Jarrett et al. 1998). Punishing children by not letting them play is not likely to improve behavior or promote learning. In many schools, recess may be the only time children are free to interact. Depriving children of recess denies them the opportunity to learn important social skills such as turn taking, sharing, and organizing.

School Through Children's Eyes: Less Playful Learning

Bowdon and Desimone (2014) compared kindergarten data from 1998 to 1999 and from 2010 to 2011, before and after implementation of the No Child Left Behind (NCLB) Act

of 2001. They found that following NCLB, children "spent less time on art, pretend play, and child-led exploration and more time on teacher-directed instruction and worksheets. Disparities between student proficiency and instructional practices for children attending schools in high and low poverty areas persisted but did not widen." In other words, less time for play and more time for direct instruction did *not* lessen the achievement gap. The following studies illustrate the effect of these trends on students.

Children's own perspectives of their school experiences support these research findings that play opportunities are not equitable. For the past 14 years, Darlene DeMarie and her students at University of South Florida have investigated how children show and tell others about their elementary school experiences. First, children are interviewed about what they do at school and what they learn there. Next, they take photographs for a book to show others what their school is like (a method known as autophotography). On another day, children do a picture selection task in which they review photographs with labels representing common themes, such as *my friends*, *the teachers*, *playing*, *having fun*, and *the school building*. (See the photograph.) Children select the one they think "best shows" others what their school is like, and the one that is the "most important" to them.

Collectively, all three methods—children's talk, photographs, and picture selections of play—reveal key differences among schools through children's eyes. In fact, the three vary depending on the racial and ethnic demographics of the children and by the socioeconomic status of the children's families.

DeMarie (2010) compared children's perceptions of their schools at a "successful" school and an "unsuccessful" school. These labels were based on Florida's statewide rating system, which used only children's scores in reading and math on a standardized achievement test, the Florida Comprehensive Assessment Test (FCAT). At the time of this research, schools with the highest achievement test scores were labeled "A" schools. Those with the lowest scores were labeled "F" schools. The "A" and "F" schools in this study were both charter schools located in urban neighborhoods that are home to high numbers of families with low incomes. However, 92 percent of the students attending the "A" charter school were White and 92 percent of students attending the "F" charter school were Black. The "F" school was a Title I school (having a high percentage of children eligible for free and reduced-price lunches), but the "A" school was not. The "A" school charged higher school fees (for items such as school uniforms and supplies), which meant that it drew a lower percentage of children from the surrounding neighborhood.

The results of that study suggested differences in children's opportunities for play in these two schools, and these differences were especially evident for children in the primary grades. Children in kindergarten to second grade attending the "A" school talked significantly more about play than similar grade-level children in the "F" school. When children attending the "F" school did mention play, it seemed it was not a typical part of their school day but something that occurred infrequently. For example, a first-grader mentioned that the class would have a party the following Friday, and that the students would have fun playing outside, eating, and "looking at cars and places." At the "A" school, 24 percent of the children in kindergarten to second grade took at least one photograph that represented play. At the "F" school, only 7 percent of the children took any photographs that represented play.

In response to the question "Which picture best shows what your school is like?," 21 percent of the "A" school children in kindergarten to second grade selected the pictures of "play" or "fun." In contrast, none of the children at the "F" school selected either of those pictures as best showing what their school was like.

The same researchers also conducted studies at schools with moderate achievement (i.e., "C" schools according to the State of Florida), again using interviews, autophotography, and picture selection to learn about children's perceptions of their school experiences. The schools had similar standardized achievement test results, but their demographics differed tremendously. Again, it was evident that opportunities for play were not equitable. Children at the school with a higher percentage of racially underrepresented groups and free or reduced-price lunch eligibility talked significantly less about play than children who attended the other school. (Tellingly, none of the children in kindergarten at either school took any photographs of play.)

Decision makers often think that schools that are not achieving need more academic instructional time. Yet the findings of this research contradict this belief. The most successful school (the "A" school) was the one that offered children more play opportunities. The least successful schools were those that did not offer children regular play opportunities. In fact, when the researchers entered the classroom at the most successful school, the children were engaged in active learning or play and hardly noticed their entry. On the other hand, not only did all the children in the least successful school

Examples of Change

One example of a program that has made a difference in the quality of outdoor play spaces is the Boston Schoolyard Initiative (www.schoolyards.org). Described in *The Great Outdoors*, revised edition, by Mary Rivkin, this initiative transformed 88 Boston Public School yards from asphalt lots to dynamic play and learning spaces. Though the initiative is no longer operative, the schoolyards continue to be inspirational places for children, and the program has also inspired similar ones such as the Oakland Schoolyard Initiative in California.

Here are further examples of initiatives that have successfully provided better play spaces for children in low-income areas:

- National Park and Recreation Association (www.nrpa.org/uploadedFiles/nrpa.org/Publications_and_Research/Research/Papers/Parks-Rec-Underserved-Areas.pdf)
- The Learning Landscapes Program, Denver (http://www.rwjf.org/en/research-publications/find-rwjf-research/2010/09/influence-of-schoolyard-renovations-on-children-s-physical-activ.html)
- Community Parks Initiative, New York (http://www1.nyc.gov/office-of-the-mayor/news/468-14/de-blasio-administration-launches-community-parks-initiative-build-more-inclusive-equitable#/0)
- KaBOOM! (kaboom.org; http://www.azcentral.com/story/news/local/glendale/2014/10/24/west-valley-cities-building-parks-low-income-areas/17827583/)

Memo to: Early Education Leaders
From: Jason Sachs, Ben Mardell, and David Ramsey
Date: January 2015
Subject: Intentional Play-Based Learning: An Essential Ingredient

You know about the research demonstrating the critical role high-quality early childhood education plays in children's academic and social success. What you might not know is that the programs on which the findings are based have an important factor in common: play. Play is an essential ingredient in children's social, emotional, intellectual, and moral development. When children play, they expand their imaginations, practice language skills, and learn to control their impulses (creating and following rules in order to keep the play going). These skills are all necessary to navigate successfully in school.

That is why, in Boston Public pre-K and kindergarten programs, we teach students using a curriculum that is based on an 80-minute block of time for students to choose where and how to participate in multiple centers. Our research demonstrates that this curriculum leads to particularly strong gains in vocabulary, executive functioning, and self-regulation, and predicts success in third grade.

Having time to process academic information through play and other forms of learning is critical for all students. It is especially important for students who have lower vocabulary levels. There is a tendency in schools that serve students predominantly on free and reduced lunch to exclude play in order to focus on literacy skill building. This strategy is counterproductive, as it does not match the way young students learn. The young brain is constructed to make connections between and across concepts. Only later do students consolidate specific knowledge—math, science, and literacy—as independent domains for learning.

We encourage you to work with your school leadership team and city planners to promote constructive, intentional play-based learning as an essential ingredient in the curriculum in all of your preschool and kindergarten programs. Our experience in Boston Public, along with hundreds of research articles on the science of how children learn, demonstrates that intentional play that allows for student choice and time to process and synthesize ensures that we set our young students up with necessary opportunities to succeed in school and become productive citizens.

Jason Sachs, EdD, is director of early childhood for Boston Public Schools. **Ben Mardell,** PhD, is professor of early education at Lesley University. **David Ramsey**, MAT, is program director in early childhood for Boston Public Schools.

notice the researchers' entry, they practically begged to be the ones who could leave their classrooms and their piles of worksheets on their desks.

Conclusion

Awareness of disparities in quality play opportunities is a first step toward advocating for children to have a quality life that includes opportunities for play. Our goal is to consider if we (as educators, therapists, and researchers) are really interested in tackling all facets of the implications of play for *all* children. Make sure the children in your setting—and those in others—have good play opportunities. For example, do all the schools in your community have safe playgrounds? Do all schools provide recess every day? Are challenging behaviors addressed through means other than depriving children of recess? Do all schools have opportunities for highly motivating and fun learning activities, such as art, music, child-led exploration, and recess?

We hope this article will lead readers to probe these issues more deeply by considering questions such as these:

- What policies and practices are in place that discriminate against or privilege particular groups of children?
- What are our inherent assumptions and prejudices regarding who deserves play?
- How does understanding social justice issues affect our perceptions of play spaces, access, and quality?
- What do we do with this information?
- How are individuals, rule makers, and rule enforcers addressing these issues?
- Who will initiate and lead a democratic play and playground movement?

We recognize that play is essential for a child's academic, social, physical, and emotional well-being. We are also aware that the quantity and quality of play children experience is heavily influenced by the social and political contexts in which such activities take place, reflecting inequities in our society. This article examines a limited range of play opportunities: playground quality, access to recess breaks, and incorporation of play and fun into the school day. We hope it has raised awareness that other areas of quality play experiences described in this book may not be available to *all* children. Play advocates, including parents, caregivers, teachers, and administrators, often become involved in these issues because of concerns about their own children or their own programs. But, for a more just and democratic society, play advocates need to act to support play opportunities for other people's children as well as their own. We hope this article has increased awareness of such needs.

References

American Academy of Pediatrics. 2013. "The Crucial Role of Recess in School." Policy statement. *Pediatrics* 131 (1): 183–88. http://pediatrics.aappublications.org/content/131/1/183.full.

Bowdon, J., & L.M. Desimone. 2014. "More Work, Less Play: Kindergarten, Post-NCLB." *Teachers College Record.* ID Number 17742.

Brown, S. 2010. *Play: How It Shapes the Brain, Opens the Imagination, and Invigorates the Soul.* New York: Avery Trade.

Centers for Disease Control and Prevention (CDC). 2010. *The Association Between School-Based Physical Activity, Including Physical Education, and Academic Performance.* US Department of Health and Human Services. www.cdc.gov/healthyyouth/health_and_academics/pdf/pa-pe_paper.pdf.

DeMarie, D. 2010. "Successful Versus Unsuccessful Schools Through the Eyes of Children: The Use of Interviews, Autophotography, and Picture Selection." *Early Childhood Research & Practice* 12 (2). http://ecrp.uiuc.edu/v12n2/demarie.html.

Gray, P. 2013. *Free To Learn: Why Unleashing the Instinct to Play Will Make Our Children Happier, More Self-Reliant, and Better Students for Life*. New York: Basic Books.

Jarrett, O.S. 2003. "Urban School Recess: The Haves and the Have Nots." *Play, Policy, & Practice Connections* 8 (1): 1–3, 7–10.

Jarrett, O.S. 2013. "A Research-Based Case for Recess." US Play Coalition in collaboration with Alliance for Childhood and the American Association for the Child's Right to Play. http://usplaycoalition.clemson.edu/resources/articles/13.11.5_Recess_final_online.pdf.

Jarrett, O.S., D. Maxwell, C. Dickerson, P. Hoge, G. Davies, & A. Yetley. 1998. "The Impact of Recess on Classroom Behavior: Group Effects and Individual Differences." *The Journal of Educational Research* 92 (2): 121–26.

Kestly, T.A. 2014. *The Interpersonal Neurobiology of Play: Brain-Building Interventions for Emotional Well-Being.* New York: W.W. Norton.

Piaget, J. 1976. *To Understand Is to Invent: The Future of Education*. London: Penguin Books.

Rivkin, M., With D. Schein. 2014. *The Great Outdoors: Advocating for Natural Spaces for Young Children.* Rev. ed. Washington, DC: NAEYC.

Roth, J.L., J. Brooks-Gunn, M.R. Linver, & S.L. Hofferth. 2002. "What Happens During the School Day? Time Diaries From a National Sample of Elementary School Teachers." *Teachers College Record.* ID Number 11018.

Vygotsky, L.S. 1980. *Mind in Society: The Development of Higher Psychological Processes*. Cambridge, MA: Harvard University Press.

Frances M. Carlson

Big Body Play: Understanding and Supporting It

Young children enjoy very physical play that is often vigorous, intense, and rough. You may know this "big body play" as *rough-and-tumble play, roughhousing, horseplay,* or *play fighting*. In its organized play forms with older children, we call it many names: King of the Mountain, Red Rover, Freeze Tag, and so on.

From infancy, children use their bodies to learn. They roll back and forth, kick their legs, and wave their arms, sometimes alone and sometimes alongside another infant. They crawl on top of each other. They use adults' bodies to stand up, push off, and launch themselves forward and backward. As toddlers, they pull each other, hug each other tightly, and push each other down. As children approach the preschool years, these very physical ways of interacting and learning begin to follow a predictable pattern of unique characteristics: running, chasing, fleeing, wrestling, open-palm tagging, swinging around, and falling to the ground—often on top of each other.

Sometimes young children's big body play is solitary. Preschoolers run around, dancing and swirling, rolling on the floor or on the ground, or hopping and skipping along. Children's rough play can include the use of objects. For example,

naeyc® 2, 3

primary children might climb up structures and then leap off, roll their bodies on large yoga balls, and sometimes tag objects as "base" for an organized game. More often, this play includes children playing with other children and making rules to accompany their rough play.

Children's big body play may resemble, but does not usually involve, real fighting (Tannock 2011). Because it may at times closely resemble actual fighting, some adults find it to be challenging behavior. In spite of its bad reputation, rough play is a valuable and viable play style from infancy through the early primary years—one that teachers and families need to understand and support.

Misconceptions About Rough Play

Teachers and parents often mistake this play style for real fighting that can lead to injury, so they prohibit it. This play style has also been neglected and sometimes criticized at both state and national levels.

The 2007 Child Development Associate (CDA) *Assessment Observation Instrument*, used to observe and evaluate a CDA candidate's classroom practices, states, "Rough play is minimized. Example: defuses rough play before it becomes a problem; makes superhero play more manageable by limiting time and place" (Council for Professional Recognition 2007, 31). In Georgia, a 2014 statewide licensing standards revision includes a rule that states, "Staff shall not engage in, or allow children or other adults to engage in, activities that could be detrimental to a child's health or well-being, such as, but not limited to, horse play, rough play, wrestling" (Bright From the Start 2014, 9). Standards or expectations like these are based on the assumption that play fighting typically escalates or that children are often injured while playing this way. However, neither assumption is true (Smith, Smees, & Pellegrini 2004).

Frances M. Carlson, MEd, is the lead instructor for the Early Childhood Care & Education department at Chattahoochee Technical College in Marietta, Georgia. She is the author of *Big Body Play: Why Boisterous, Vigorous, and Very Physical Play Is Essential to Children's Development and Learning* (NAEYC).

When play fighting does escalate, escalation typically occurs when participants include children who have been rejected (Smith, Smees, & Pellegrini 2004). (Children who are rejected are those "actively avoided by peers. These peers are named often as undesirable playmates" [Trawick-Smith 2014, 317].)

Attempts to ban or control children's big body play are intended to protect children, but such attempts are ill placed because children's rough play has different components and consequences from real fighting (Tannock 2011). Rather than forbidding rough-and-tumble play, which can aid in increasing a child's social skills, teachers' and parents' efforts are better directed toward supporting and supervising this type of play, so that young children's social skills and friendship-making skills can develop (Pellis & Pellis 2007).

Programs that operate under guidelines that forbid roughhousing because of the misconception that it is fighting or fears that it will inevitably lead to injury should work to educate stakeholders and decision makers. Provide them with resources about the myriad benefits of rough play. Document the learning involved when children play this way, and share your documentation (photographs, anecdotal notes, standards correlations) with families and others.

What It Is and What It Is Not

Big body play is distinctly different from fighting. Fighting includes physical acts used to coerce or control another person, either through inflicting pain or through the threat of pain. Real fighting involves tears instead of laughter and closed fists instead of open palms (Fry 2005). When open palms are used in real fighting, it is for a slap instead of a tag. When two children are fighting, usually one runs away as soon as possible and does not voluntarily return for more. With some practice, teachers and parents can learn to discern children's appropriate big body play from inappropriate real fighting.

In appropriate rough play, children's faces are free and easy, their muscle tone is relaxed, and they are usually smiling and laughing (Tannock 2011). In real fighting, the facial movements are rigid, controlled, stressed, and the jaw is usually clenched (Fry 2005). In rough play, children initiate the play and sustain it by taking turns. In real fighting, one child usually dominates another child (or children) and the other child may be in the situation against his or her will. In rough play, the children return for more even if it seems too rough to adult onlookers. In real fighting, children run away, sometimes in tears, and often ask the teacher or another adult for help.

Why It Matters

Rough-and-tumble play provides invaluable opportunities for learning. According to NAEYC (2009), "development and learning advance when children are challenged to achieve at a level just beyond their current mastery, and also when they have many opportunities to practice newly acquired skills" (15). Children's rough body play provides these necessary challenges and opportunities. Through their rough play, they are building a range of skills representing every developmental domain. For example, children learn physical skills—how their bodies move and how to control their movements. They also develop language skills through signals and nonverbal communication, including the ability to perceive, infer, and decode. Children develop social skills through taking turns, playing dominant and subordinate roles, negotiating, and developing and maintaining friendships (Lindsey & Colwell 2013). For boys in particular, rough play provides a venue for showing care and concern as they often hug and pat each other on the back during and after the play (Reed 2005). Rough play also allows young children to have

In appropriate rough play, children's faces are free and easy, their muscle tone is relaxed, and they are usually smiling and laughing.

their physical touch needs met in individually and age-appropriate ways (Reed 2005; Carlson 2006) and provides an opportunity for children to take healthy risks.

Rough play allows children to practice adult roles. That is, such play helps prepare children for the complex social aspects of adult life (Pellegrini, Dupuis, & Smith 2007). Other researchers speculate that it is practice for future self-defense, providing vital skills and the development of critical pathways in the brain for adaptive responses to aggression and dominance (Pellis & Pellis 2007). There is a known connection between the development of movement and the development of cognition (Cook et al. 2012), and researchers believe there is a connection between this very physical, rowdy play style and critical periods of brain development (Gordon et al. 2003). Rough play between peers appears to be critical for learning how to calibrate movements and orient oneself physically in appropriate and adaptive ways (Sandseter 2011). There is evidence that rough-and-tumble play leads to the release of chemicals affecting the mid-brain, lower forebrain, and the cortex, including areas responsible for decision making and social discrimination; growth chemicals positively affect development of these brain areas (Pellis & Pellis 2007). In other words, rough-and-tumble play, this universal children's activity, is adaptive, evolutionarily useful, and linked to normal brain development.

Supporting Rough Play

One of the best ways teachers can support rough play is by modeling it for children. For example, two teachers might show children the required hand positions for wrestling—below the neck and above the waist—by placing their hands on each other in these positions. When adults model high levels of vigorous activity, such as running, the children in their care are more likely to play this way. Children also play more vigorously and more productively when their teachers have formal education or training in the importance of this type of play (Cardon et al. 2008).

Besides modeling, teachers can do three specific things to provide for and support rough play while minimizing the potential for injury: prepare both the indoor and outdoor environment, develop and implement policies and rules for rough play, and supervise rough play so they can intervene when appropriate.

Environments That Support Big Body Play

The learning environment should provide rich opportunities for children to use their bodies both indoors and outdoors (Curtis & Carter 2005). Natural playground environments afford children greater opportunities for rough play as they typically provide elements like boulders, logs, stumps, and hills in varying degrees of steepness (Sandseter 2009). When planning for big, rough, vigorous body play, give keen, thoughtful attention to potential safety hazards. Children need to play vigorously with their bodies, but they must do so in a safe setting.

To support rough play with infants during floor time, provide safe, mouthable objects in a variety of shapes, colors, and textures. Place the items near to and away from the baby to encourage reaching and stretching. Also provide a variety of large items—inclined hollow blocks, large rubber balls, sturdy tubes, exercise mats—so infants can roll on, around, over, and on top of these items. Get on the floor, too, so infants can crawl around and lie on you. Allow babies to be near each other so that they can play with each other's bodies. Supervise their play to allow for safe exploration.

Indoor environments encourage big body play when there is ample space for children to move around freely. Cramped or restricted areas hamper children's vigorous play. When usable space is less than 25 square feet per child, children tend to be more aggressive (Ferguson et al. 2013). Boys, especially, tend to play more actively when more space is available (Cardon et al. 2008).

Some teachers find it helpful to define a particular section of the room and dedicate it to big body play. One teacher shares the way she established a "wrestling zone" in her preschool classroom:

> First, I cleared the area of any furniture or equipment. Next, I defined the area with a thick, heavy comforter and pillows. After setting up the area, I posted guidelines for the children's rough play on the wall near the wrestling zone.

Designate an area for rough play where there is no nearby furniture or equipment with sharp points and corners. Firmly anchor furniture so that it doesn't upturn if a child pushes against it. All flooring should be skid-free, with safety surfaces like thick mats to absorb the shock of any potential impact.

Rough-and-tumble play, this universal children's activity, is adaptive, evolutionarily useful, and linked to normal brain development.

Policies and Rules for Rough Play

Programs need policies about rough play. Policies should define this type of play, explain rules that accompany it, specify the level of supervision it requires, and include specific types of staff development or training early childhood teachers need to support it. In addition, policies can address how to include it in the schedule and how to make sure all children—especially children with developmental disabilities and children who are socially rejected—have access to it. Clear policies about supervision are vital, as this play style requires constant adult supervision—meaning the children are both seen and heard at all times by supervising adults. According to NAEYC (2010), "lapses in supervision of children can happen in all types of programs, and even a momentary lapse can

Families and Play

Families often wonder if they should let their children engage in physical, vigorous, boisterous play. My husband and I asked ourselves this same question when our children were young, and we decided to support the rough play because many of our own happiest childhood memories revolved around it. I'm glad we made that decision, because this play style also furthers children's physical, social, emotional, and cognitive development.

Research suggests that children who have roughhoused may be smarter than children who have not (Stevens et al. 2008; Tomporowski et al. 2008). This is partly due to changes in brain chemistry that result from rough play, and partly because rough play results in longer periods of focused calm, which may allow children to better attend to cognitive activities.

Share these points with families about rough play:

- Rough play is rowdy, physical, and usually very loud. It looks a lot like fighting, but it isn't. Rough play rarely turns into real fighting.
- The quickest way to discern rough play from real fighting is by the children's facial expressions: Their smiles let us know the play is okay.
- Rough play is a vital component of children's growth and development, and it positively impacts every area of learning.
    - The physical advantage of engaging in rough play is obvious: When children are running back and forth, chasing and fleeing, jumping and leaping, rolling and bouncing, they are building strong, healthy bodies. Roughhousing gives children the sustained moderate-to-vigorous physical exercise they need to remain fit and healthy. Such activity also helps children focus better; they are typically calmer after about 10 minutes of rough play.
    - When children play roughly with each other, they have to compromise for the play to continue. Rough play generally involves rules about who goes first, what makes someone the winner, and how rough the children can be with each other without actually inflicting any physical pain. That means the children are learning to take turns, share, and hold back in order to sustain the play.
    - Children also learn to understand each other's nonverbal communication when roughhousing, such as motioning, waving, pointing, grunting, and squeezing tighter or pushing away. Children with strong nonverbal skills roughhouse with ease. For children who need to improve their reading of others' nonverbal cues, rough play is a good way for them to learn these skills.

Offer these suggestions to families who want to support their children's big body play:

- Talk with your children and together set ground rules for their rough play.
- Supervise play closely and assist children in their verbal and nonverbal communication as they play.
- Rough play with your children—both boys and girls!—but do not dominate them and don't let them dominate you. The play should remain equal. They'll see that sometimes holding back is important.

References

Stevens, T.A., Y. To, S.J. Stevenson, & M.R. Lochbaum. 2008. "The Importance of Physical Activity and Physical Education in the Prediction of Academic Achievement." *Journal of Sport Behavior* 31 (4): 368–88.

Tomporowski, P.D., C.L. Davis, P.H. Miller, & J.A. Naglieri. 2008. "Exercise and Children's Intelligence, Cognition, and Academic Achievement." *Educational Psychology Review* 20 (2): 111–31.

have disastrous consequences. When a lapse occurs that affects program quality and puts children at risk, it is critical to consider the nature of the incident and its lessons for future risk management" (1).

Even with its friendly nature and ability to build and increase children's social skills, this play style is more productive and manageable when guidelines and rules are in place. Children can help create the rules. By preschool age, children are learning about and can begin participating in games with rules. Involving the children in creating rules for their play supports this emerging ability.

The rules should apply to children's roughhousing as well as to big body play with equipment and play materials. Wrestling, for example, may have rules such as wrestling only while kneeling, and arms around shoulders to waists but not around necks or heads. For big body play with equipment, the rules may state that the slide can be used for climbing on alternate days with sliding, or that a child can climb up the slide only after checking to make sure no one is sliding down, and that jumping can be from stationary structures only and never from swings. Other rules may say that tumbling indoors always requires a mat and cannot be done on a bare floor, and that children may only roll down hills that are fenced or away from streets and traffic.

Some general rules for big body play might be

- No hitting
- No pinching
- Hands below the neck and above the waist
- Stop as soon as the other person says or signals stop
- No rough play while standing—kneeling only
- Rough play is optional—stop and leave when you want (A Place of Our Own 2014)

Write the rules on white poster board, and mount them near the designated rough play area.

Supervise and Intervene

Teachers should enforce the rules and step in to ensure all children are safe, physically and emotionally. It's important to pay attention to children's language during rough play and help them use words to express some of the nonverbal communication. For example, if two boys are playing and one is on top of the other, say, "He is pushing against your chest! He wants you to get up!" Help the larger boy get up if he needs assistance. Instead of scolding, simply point out, "Because you are larger than he is, I think he felt uncomfortable with you on top of him." Encourage the smaller boy to say these words, too. Help

Sample Handbook Policies for Big Body Play

Big Body Play for Preschool and School-Age Children

Here at [name of school or program], we believe in the value of exuberant, boisterous, rough-and-tumble play to a child's overall development. This vigorous body play allows children opportunities to use language—both verbal and nonverbal—and learn how to negotiate, take turns, wait, compromise, sometimes dominate and sometimes hold back, and make and follow rules. They are learning about cause and effect and developing empathy. Big body play also supports optimum physical development because it is so vigorous and because children—since they enjoy it so much—tend to engage in it for an extended amount of time.

To support the use of big body play, we do the following:

- Provide training to all staff on the importance of big body play and how to supervise it
- Prepare both indoor and outdoor environments for this play style
- Establish classroom and playground rules with the children to keep them safe and help them know what to expect
- Encourage staff to use big body games with the children
- Supervise the play constantly, which means ensuring an adult is watching and listening at all times
- Model appropriate play; coach children as they play so that they are able to interact comfortably with each other in this way

The following indoor and outdoor environmental features of our program support big body play:

- At least 50 square feet of usable indoor play space per child, free from furniture and equipment so that children can tumble and wrestle (e.g., a wrestling area for two children would consist of at least 100 square feet with no furnishings in the area)
- At least 100 square feet of usable outdoor play space per child, free from fixed equipment so that children can run, jump, tag, roll, wrestle, twirl, fall down, and chase each other (e.g., a group of six children playing tag would have at least 600 square feet in which to play)
- Safety surfaces indoors under and around climbers, and furniture that children might use as climbers (a loveseat, e.g.,)
- Safety surfaces outdoors under and around climbers, slides, balance beams, and other elevated surfaces from which children might jump

From F.M. Carlson, *Big Body Play: Why Boisterous, Vigorous, and Very Physical Play Is Essential to Children's Development and Learning* (Washington, DC: NAEYC 2011), 87–88. © NAEYC.

children problem solve about ways to accommodate their size differences if they are unable to do so unassisted. Say, "How else can you wrestle so that one of you isn't pinned under the other one?"

When supervising children with less developed social skills, remember that for these children, big body play can more easily turn into real fighting. Many children who are socially rejected lack the awareness and language skills needed to correctly interpret body signals and body language, which makes rough play difficult for them. The children often lack the social skill of turn taking or reciprocity. A child may feel challenged or threatened by another child's movement or action instead of understanding that rough play involves give-and-take and that he or she will also get a turn.

Although more difficult for them, engaging in big body play can help such children build social skills. When supervising these children, remain closer to them than you would to other children. If you see or sense that a child may be misunderstanding cues or turn taking, intervene. Help clarify the child's understanding of the play so it can continue. Strategies like coaching, helping the child reflect on cues and responses, and explaining and modeling sharing and reciprocity help a child remain in the play and ultimately support his or her language and social competence.

Children with disabilities or developmental delays tend to play more passively; they watch more and initiate less. However, children with special needs often have the same preferences for active play and the same developmental need for physical challenges (Case-Smith & Kuhaneck 2008). Make sure opportunities for big body play are available for *all* children by providing active supervision and supporting each child's attempts to use his body in new and challenging ways.

Consider each child's needs and how she might respond to the situation. For example, a child with cognitive disabilities may need assistance understanding the rules associated with roughhousing. Children with speech and language deficits may have difficulty using the verbal and nonverbal language their peers use to negotiate, take turns, and communicate that the activity has become too vigorous for them. Children with emotional and behavior disorders may need greater support when they are involved in close physical contact with other children. Be very aware of each child's capabilities and what assistance is needed, and work closely with support staff to ensure that the environment and activities are appropriate and allow for children's full participation.

When Landry flipped Taylor over onto his back, Taylor stopped laughing and scrunched his face in a grimace. Landry let go of Taylor and Taylor got up. I asked Landry, "How did you know to let go?" Landry replied, "I could just tell."

Communicating With Families

Some children already feel that their rough body play is watched too closely by their early childhood teachers (Tannock 2008). Not all parents, though, find children's rough play unacceptable. Some feel that rough play is empowering for their daughters, and they appreciate how this play style makes their girls feel strong ("Preschoolers and Rough and Tumble Play" 2008). Rough play is the most common play style not only in nonhuman animals but in humans as well, with children in industrialized countries and children in many other cultures playing this way (Sandseter 2011).

If children learn that rough play is acceptable at home but not at school, it may be difficult for them to understand and comply with school rules. Children are better able to reap the benefits of rough play when both home and school have consistent rules and messages. Children thrive in early childhood programs where administrators, teachers, and family members work together in partnerships (Keyser 2006). Partnership is crucial for children to feel supported in their big body play.

Children are better able to reap the benefits of rough play when both home and school have consistent rules and messages.

Teachers who decide to offer big body play must make sure that families are aware of and understand why rough play is included. Communicate program components to families when they first express interest in the program or at events such as an open house before the first day of school. Explain the use of and support for big body play in a variety of ways:

- Include in your family handbook a policy on big body play—and how it is supported and supervised in the program or school (see "Sample Handbook Policies for Big Body Play" on p. 114).
- Send a letter to families that explains big body play and its many benefits.
- Show photographs of children engaged in big body play
    - —In newsletters
    - —In documentation panels (a virtual or physical display of photographs, captions, anecdotal notes, etc.)
    - —In promotional literature, such as brochures and flyers
    - —On bulletin boards at entryways

Memo to: The Early Childhood Education Community
From: Rae Pica
Date: January 2015
Subject: Eat, Sleep, Breathe, and Play

Children are *born* to play in much the same way that kittens and puppies are born to play. Play is open ended and intrinsically motivated. It is joyful, self-directed, and focused on process, not goals. This is true play.

Children learn essential skills through play, including the social skills of sharing, cooperating, negotiating, compromising, making and revising rules, and taking the perspective of others. True play provides opportunities for children to meet and solve problems—the number-one ability they will most assuredly require in a rapidly changing world. Play helps children express their thoughts and feelings, deal with stress, and cope with fears they can't yet understand or articulate.

Through play, children acquire literacy, mathematical, and creative skills. Make-believe play, in particular, has been linked to self-regulation skills, which in turn have been associated with greater academic success than has IQ. Self-regulation also helps children gain self-control and manage stress while learning. A playful attitude is a critical life skill, and we are more likely to retain it as adults if, as children, we engaged in playful exploration.

When we see children play and learn, we have daily evidence of the value of play. It is a need no different or less important than their need to eat, sleep, and breathe. For young children, play is every bit as essential.

Rae Pica speaks and writes about developmentally appropriate practice and the education of the whole child.

Going Forward

Most children engage in rough play, and research demonstrates its physical, social, emotional, and cognitive value. Early childhood education settings have the responsibility to provide children with what best serves their developmental needs. When children successfully participate in big body play, it is "a measure of the children's social well-being and is marked by the ability of children to . . . cooperate, to lead, and to follow" (Burdette & Whitaker 2005, 48). These abilities don't just support big body play; these skills are necessary for lifelong success in relationships.

References

A Place of Our Own. 2014. "Rough Play Area." Accessed October 21. www.aplaceofourown.org/activity.php?id=492.

Bright From the Start, Georgia Department of Early Care and Learning. 2014. *Rules for Child Care Learning Centers: Chapter 591-1-1.* h http://nrckids.org/default/assets/File/StateRegs/GA/CCLCRulesandRegulations.pdf.

Burdette, H.L., & R.C. Whitaker. 2005. "Resurrecting Free Play in Young Children: Looking Beyond Fitness and Fatness to Attention, Affiliation, and Affect." *Archives of Pediatrics & Adolescent Medicine* 159 (1): 46–50.

Cardon, G., E. Van Cauwenberghe, V. Labarque, L. Haerens, & I. De Bourdeaudhuij. 2008. "The Contribution of Preschool Playground Factors in Explaining Children's Physical Activity During Recess." *International Journal of Behavioral Nutrition and Physical Activity* 5 (11): 1186–192.

Carlson, F.M. 2006. *Essential Touch: Meeting the Needs of Young Children.* Washington, DC: NAEYC.

Case-Smith, J., & H.M. Kuhaneck. 2008. "Play Preferences of Typically Developing Children and Children With Developmental Delays Betweeen Ages 3 and 7 Years." *Occupational Therapy Journal of Research* 28 (1): 19–29.

Cook, A.M., K. Adams, P. Encarnacao, & L. Alvarez. 2012. "The Role of Assisted Manipulation in Cognitive Development." *Developmental Neurorehabilitation* 15 (2): 136–48.

Council for Professional Recognition. 2007. "Methods for Avoiding Problems Are Implemented." *CDA Assessment Observation Instrument.* Washington, DC: Council for Professional Recognition.

Curtis, D., & M. Carter. 2005. "Rethinking Early Childhood Environments to Enhance Learning." *Young Children* 60 (3): 34–38.

Ferguson, K.T., R.C. Cassells, J.W. MacAllister, & G.W. Evans. 2013. "The Physical Environment and Child Development: An International Review." *International Journal of Pscyhology* 48 (4): 437–68.

Fry, D.P. 2005. "Rough-and-Tumble Social Play in Humans." In *The Nature of Play: Great Apes and Humans,* eds. A.D. Pellegrini & P.K. Smith, 54–85. New York: Guilford Press.

Gordon, N.S., S. Burke, H. Akil, S.J. Watson, & J. Panksepp. 2003. "Socially-Induced Brain 'Fertilization': Play Promotes Brain Derived Neurotrophic Factor Transcription in the Amygdala and Dorsolateral Frontal Cortex in Juvenile Rats." *Neuroscience Letters* 341 (1): 17–20.

Keyser, J. 2006. *From Parents to Partners: Building a Family-Centered Early Childhood Program.* St. Paul, MN: Redleaf; Washington, DC: NAEYC.

Lindsey, E.W., & M.J. Colwell. 2013. "Pretend and Physical Play: Links to Preschoolers' Affective Social Competence." *Merrill-Palmer Quarterly* 59 (3): 330–60.

NAEYC. 2009. "Developmentally Appropriate Practice in Early Childhood Programs Serving Children From Birth Through Age 8." Position statement. www.naeyc.org/positionstatements/dap.

NAEYC. 2010. "Lessons From NAEYC Accreditation: Avoiding Lapses in Supervision That Place Children at Risk." *Young Children* 65 (2): 78–80.

Paquette, D., R. Carbonneau, D. Dubeau, M. Bigras, & R.E. Tremblay. 2003. "Prevalence of Father-Child Rough-and-Tumble Play and Physical Aggression in Preschool Children." *European Journal of Psychology of Education* 18 (2): 171–89.

Pellegrini, A.D., D. Dupuis, & P.K. Smith. 2007. "Play in Evolution and Development." *Developmental Review* 27: 261–76.

Pellis, S.M., & V.C. Pellis. 2007. "Rough-and-Tumble Play and the Development of the Social Brain."*Current Directions in Psychological Science* 16 (2): 95–98.

"Preschoolers and Rough and Tumble Play." Ontario: TVO, 2008. Video, 10 min. www.tvo.org/TVO/WebObjects/TVO.woa?videoid?24569407001. [Can be viewed at http://scriptnc.fpg.unc.edu/resources/preschoolers-and-rough-and-tumble-play.]

Reed, T.L. 2005. "A Qualitative Approach to Boys' Rough and Tumble Play: There Is More Than Meets the Eye." In *Play: An Interdisciplinary Synthesis,* eds. F.F. McMahon, D.E. Lytle, & B. Sutton-Smith, 53–71. Lanham, MD: University Press of America.

Sandseter, E.B.H. 2009. "Affordances for Risky Play in Preschool: The Importance of Features in the Play Environment." *Early Childhood Education Journal* 36 (5): 439–46.

Sandseter, E.B.H. 2011. "Children's Risky Play From an Evolutionary Perspective: The Anti-Phobic Effects of Thrilling Experiences." *Evolutionary Psychology* 9 (2): 257–84.

Smith, P.K., R. Smees, & A.D. Pellegrini. 2004. "Play Fighting and Real Fighting: Using Video Playback Methodology with Young Children." *Aggressive Behavior* 30 (2): 164–73.

Tannock, M.T. 2008. "Rough and Tumble Play: An Investigation of the Perceptions of Educators and Young Children." *Early Childhood Education Journal* 35 (4): 357–61.

Tannock, M.T. 2011. "Observing Young Children's Rough-and-Tumble Play." *Australasian Journal of Early Childhood* 36 (2): 13–20.

Trawick-Smith, J. 2014. *Early Childhood Development: A Multicultural Perspective.* 6th ed. Upper Saddle River, NJ: Pearson Merrill Prentice Hall.

Resources for Supporting Young Children's Play

NAEYC Resources

Carlson, F.M. 2011. *Big Body Play: Why Boisterous, Vigorous, and Very Physical Play Is Essential to Children's Development and Learning.* Washington, DC: NAEYC.

Cerniglia, E. 2013. "Musical Play in Early Childhood Classrooms: Taking It One Step Further." *Young Children* 68 (5): 68–73.

Colker, L.J. 2014. "A Place for Mud Play." Enhancing Learning Centers. *Teaching Young Children* 7 (3): 16–17.

Collins, K.M., C.J. Griess, K. Carithers, & D.M. Castillo. 2011. "It's All in the Game: Designing and Playing Board Games to Foster Communication and Social Skills." *Young Children* 66 (2): 12–19.

Drew, W.F., J. Christie, J.E. Johnson, A.M. Meckley, & M.L. Nell. 2008. "Constructive Play: A Value-Added Strategy for Meeting Early Learning Standards." *Young Children* 63 (4): 38–44.

Evitt, M.F. 2014. "Ready, Set, Learn! We're Off to the Moon." *Teaching Young Children* 7 (3): 22–25.

Ganz, J.B., & M.M. Flores. 2010. "Implementing Visual Cues for Young Children With Autism Spectrum Disorder and Their Playmates." *Young Children* 65 (3): 78–83.

Gillespie, L.G. 2009. "Why Do Babies Like Boxes Best?" BTJ. *Young Children* on the Web (May): 1–2.

Haupt, M. 2007. "Teachers on Teaching: The Value of Play." *Young Children* 62 (2): 94–95.

Hirsch, E.S., ed. 1996. *The Block Book.* 3rd ed. Washington, DC: NAEYC.

Honig, A.S. 2007. "Play: Ten Power Boosts for Children's Early Learning." *Young Children* 62 (5): 72–78.

Honig, A.S. 2015. *Experiencing Nature With Young Children: Awakening Delight, Curiosity, and a Sense of Stewardship.* Washington, DC: NAEYC.

Howell, J. 2014. "Following Your Passion: Introducing Young Children to Basketball." *Teaching Young Children* 6 (4): 10–13.

Jarrett, O., & S. Waite-Stupiansky. 2009. "Recess: It's Indispensable!" On Our Minds. *Young Children* 64 (5): 66–68.

Jones, E. 2011. "Play Across the Lifecycle: From Initiative to Integrity to Transcendence." *Young Children* 66 (4): 84–91.

Kern, P., & L. Wakeford. 2007. "Supporting Outdoor Play for Young Children: The Zone Model of Playground Supervision." *Young Children* 62 (5): 12–18.

Mardell, B., & B. Carpenter. 2012. "Places to Play in Providence: Valuing Preschool Children as Citizens." *Young Children* 67 (5): 76–78.

McDermott, L.B. 2012. "Play School: Where Children and Families Learn and Grow Together." *Young Children* 67 (2): 81–86.

Miles, L.R. 2009. "The General Store: Reflections on Children at Play." *Young Children* 64 (4): 36–41.

NAEYC. 2010. "9x: Cooperative Games for Preschoolers." Collage. *Teaching Young Children* 4 (2): 6–7.

Nell, M.L., & W.F. Drew, With D. Bush. 2013. *From Play to Practice: Connecting Teachers' Play to Children's Learning.* Washington, DC: NAEYC.

Nell, M.L., W.F. Drew, B. Rankin, B. Merrill, E. Klugman, & G. Simmons. 2011. "NAEYC Affiliate Successes: Building Play Leadership and Advocacy." *Young Children* 66 (1): 64–67.

O'Neill, B.E. 2013. "Improvisational Play Interventions: Fostering Social-Emotional Development in Inclusive Classrooms." *Young Children* 68 (3): 62–69.

Ostrosky, M.M., & H. Meadan. 2010. "Helping Children Play and Learn Together." *Young Children* 65 (1): 104–10.

Petty, K. 2009. "Using Guided Participation to Support Young Children's Social Development." *Young Children* 64 (4): 80–85.

Prairie, A.P. 2013. "Supporting Sociodramatic Play in Ways That Enhance Academic Learning." *Young Children* 68 (2): 62–68.

Ranck, E.R., & C. Anderson. 2010. "Blocks: A Versatile Learning Tool for Yesterday, Today, and Tomorrow." Our Proud Heritage. *Young Children* 65 (2): 64–56.

Riojas-Cortez, M. 2011. "Culture, Play, and Family: Supporting Young Children on the Autism Spectrum." *Young Children* 66 (5): 94–99.

Rivkin, M.S., with D. Schein. 2014. *The Great Outdoors: Providing Natural Spaces for Young Children*. Rev. ed. Washington, DC: NAEYC.

Rogers, L., & D. Steffan. 2009. "Teachers on Teaching. Clay Play." *Young Children* 64 (3): 78–81.

Swartz, M.I. 2005. "Playdough: What's Standard About It?" *Young Children* 60 (2): 100–109.

Tunks, K.W. 2013. "Happy 100th Birthday, Unit Blocks!" *Young Children* 68 (5): 82–87.

Other Articles, Books, and Additional Resources

Almon, J. 2013. "The Value of Play in Early Education, and How to Get Teachers on Board." *Principal* Sept/Oct.

Ashiabi, G.S. 2007. "Play in the Preschool Classroom: Its Socioemotional Significance and the Teacher's Role in Play." *Early Childhood Education Journal* 35 (2): 199–207. Leadershiplinc.

Bentley, D.F. 2013. *Everyday Artists: Inquiry and Creativity in the Early Childhood Classroom.* New York: Teachers College Press. Available from NAEYC.

Brown, S., & C. Vaughn. 2009. *Play: How It Shapes the Brain, Opens the Imagination, and Invigorates the Soul.* New York: Avery.

Campbell, P.H., S.A. Milbourne, & A.A. Kennedy. 2012. *CARA's Kit for Toddlers: Creating Adaptations for Routines and Activities*. Book and CD. Baltimore: Brookes. Available from NAEYC.

Casey, T. 2010. *Inclusive Play: Practical Strategies for Children From Birth to Eight.* 2nd ed. Thousand Oaks, CA: SAGE.

Cohen, L., & S. Waite-Stupiansky, eds. 2011. *Play: A Polyphony of Research, Theory, and Issues.* Play and Culture Studies, Vol. 12. The Association for the Study of Play.

Cross, A. 2010. *Come and Play: Sensory-Integration Strategies for Children With Play Challenges*. St. Paul, MN: Redleaf. Available from NAEYC.

Daly, L., & M. Beloglovsky. 2015. *Loose Parts: Inspiring Play in Young Children.* St. Paul, MN: Redleaf. Available from NAEYC.

DiCarlo, C.F., & L. Vagianos. 2009. "Using Child Preferences to Increase Play Across Interest Centers in Inclusive Early Childhood Classrooms." *Young Exceptional Children* 12 (4): 31–39.

Ebbeck, M., & M. Waniganayake. 2010. *Play in Early Childhood Education: Learning in Diverse Contexts.* New York: Oxford University Press.

Elkind, D. 2006. "The Values of Outdoor Play." *Exchange* Sept/Oct: 6–8.

Elkind, D. 2007. *The Power of Play: Learning What Comes Naturally.* Philadelphia, PA: Da Capo Press.

Frost, J.F., S.C. Wortham, & S. Reifel. 2012. *Play and Child Development.* 4th ed. Upper Saddle River, NJ: Pearson.

Ginsburg, K.R. 2007. "The Importance of Play in Promoting Healthy Child Development and Maintaining Strong Parent–Child Bonds." *Pediatrics* 119 (1): 182–91.

Gray, P. 2013. *Free to Learn: Why Unleashing the Instinct to Play Will Make Our Children Happier, More Self-Reliant, and Better Students for Life.* New York: Basic Books.

Gronlund, G. 2010. *Developmentally Appropriate Play: Guiding Young Children to a Higher Level*. St. Paul, MN: Redleaf.

Gross, C.M. 2012. "Science Concepts Young Children Learn Through Water Play." *Dimensions of Early Childhood* 40 (2): 3–12.

Gross, S., & R.C. Sanderson. 2012. "Play Is the Way." *Exchange* Sept/Oct: 50–53.

Heidemann, S., & D. Hewitt. 2009. *Play: The Pathway From Theory to Practice*. St. Paul, MN: Redleaf.

Heidemann, S., & D. Hewitt. 2014. *When Play Isn't Easy: Helping Children Enter and Sustain Play.* St. Paul, MN: Redleaf.

Henig, R.M. 2008. "Taking Play Seriously." *New York Times,* February 17.

Hirschland, D. 2009. "Addressing Social, Emotional, and Behavioral Challenges Through Play: Early Childhood Mental Health Consultation in Action." *ZERO TO THREE* 30 (1): 12–17.

Hirsh-Pasek, K., & R.M. Golinkoff. 2011. "The Great Balancing Act: Optimizing Core Curricula Through Playful Pedagogy." Chap. 15 in *The Pre-K Debates: Current Controversies and Issues,* eds. E. Zigler, W.S. Gilliam, & W.S. Barnett, pp. 110–15. Baltimore, MD: Brookes.

Hirsh-Pasek, K., R.M. Golinkoff, L.E. Berk, & D. Singer. 2008. *A Mandate for Playful Learning in Preschool: Presenting the Evidence*. New York: Oxford University Press.

Huff, M.J. 2011. *Story Play: Building Language and Literacy One Story at a Time.* Lewisville, NC: Gryphon House.

Hyson, M. 2008. *Enthusiastic and Engaged Learners: Approaches to Learning in the Early Childhood Classroom.* New York: Teachers College Press; Washington, DC: NAEYC.

Isbell, C. 2010. *Everyday Play: Fun Games to Develop the Fine Motor Skills Your Child Needs for School.* Lewisville, NC: Gryphon House.

Jacobs, G., & K. Crowley. 2007. *Play, Projects, and Preschool Standards: Nurturing Children's Sense of Wonder and Joy in Learning.* Thousand Oaks, CA: Corwin. Available from NAEYC.

Jamison, K.R., L.D. Forston, & T.L. Stanton-Chapman. 2012. "Encouraging Social Skill Development Through Play in Early Childhood Special Education Classrooms." *Young Exceptional Children* 15 (2): 3–19.

Johnson, J.A., & D. Dinger. 2014. *Let's Play: (Un) Curriculum Early Learning Adventures.* St. Paul, MN: Redleaf.

Johnson, J.E., & J.F. Christie. 2009. "Play and Digital Media." *Computers in the Schools* 26 (4): 284–89.

Jones, E., & G. Reynolds. 2011. *The Play's the Thing: Teachers' Roles in Children's Play.* 2nd ed. New York: Teachers College Press.

Krakowski, P. 2012. "Museum Superheroes: The Role of Play in Young Children's Lives." *Journal of Museum Education* 37 (1): 49–58.

Krechevsky, M., B. Mardell, M. Rivard, & D. Wilson. 2013. *Visible Learners: Promoting Reggio-Inspired Approaches in All Schools.* San Francisco: Jossey-Bass.

Levin, D.E., & N. Carlsson-Paige. 2006. *The War Play Dilemma: What Every Parent and Teacher Needs to Know.* 2nd ed. New York: Teachers College Press.

Miller, E., & J. Almon. 2009. *Crisis in the Kindergarten: Why Children Need to Play in School Education.* College Park, MD: Alliance for Childhood.

Myck-Wayne, J. 2010. "In Defense of Play: Beginning the Dialog About the Power of Play." *Young Exceptional Children* 13 (4): 14–23.

Ostroff, W.L. 2012. *Understanding How Young Children Learn: Bringing the Science of Child Development to the Classroom.* Alexandria, VA: ASCD.

Paley, V.G. 2004. *A Child's Work: The Importance of Fantasy Play.* Chicago: University of Chicago Press.

Paley, V.G. 2010. *The Boy on the Beach: Building Community Through Play.* Chicago: University of Chicago Press.

Paley, V.G. 2014. *Boys and Girls: Superheroes in the Doll Corner.* New ed. Chicago: University of Chicago Press.

Phillips, N., & L. Beavan. 2012. *Teaching Play to Children With Autism: Practical Interventions Using Identiplay.* 2nd ed. Thousand Oaks, CA: SAGE.

Pica, R. 2006. *Great Games for Young Children: Over 100 Games to Develop Self-Confidence, Problem-Solving Skills, and Cooperation.* Beltsville, MD: Gryphon House.

Redleaf, R. 2008. *Learn and Play the Green Way: Fun Activities With Reusable Materials.* St. Paul, MN: Redleaf.

Reifel, S. 2014. "Developmental Play in the Classroom." In *Handbook of Play and Learning in Early Childhood,* eds. L. Brooker, M. Blaise, & S. Edwards, 157–168). London: Sage.

Saracho, O.N. 2010. "Children's Play in the Visual Arts and Literature." *Early Child Development and Care* 180 (7): 947–56.

Saracho, O.N. 2011. *An Integrated Play-Based Curriculum for Young Children.* New York: Routledge.

Sheridan, M., J. Howard, & D. Alderson. 2011. *Play in Early Childhood: From Birth to Six Years.* 3rd ed. New York: Routledge.

Sherwood, S.A.S., & S. Reifel. 2010. "The Multiple Meanings of Play: Exploring Preservice Teachers' Beliefs About a Central Element of Early Childhood Education." *Journal of Early Childhood Teacher Education* 31: 322–43.

Sherwood, S.A.S., & S. Reifel. 2013. "Valuable and Unessential: The Paradox of Preservice Teachers' Beliefs About the Role of Play in Learning." *Journal of Research in Childhood Education* 27 (3): 267–82.

Singer, D.G., K. Hirsh-Pasek, & R.M. Golinkoff. 2006. *Play = Learning: How Play Motivates and Enhances Children's Cognitive and Social-Emotional Growth.* New York: Oxford University Press.

Smilansky. S. & L. Shefatya. 1990. *Facilitating Play: A Medium for Promoting Cognitive, Socio-Emotional, and Academic Development in Young Children.* Gaithersburg, MD: Psychological and Educational Publications.

Stephens, K. 2009. "Imaginative Play During Childhood: Required for Reaching Full Potential." *Exchange 186 (*Mar/Apr): 53–56.

Stockall, N., & L. Dennis. 2013. "Fathers' Role in Play: Enhancing Early Language and Literacy of Children With Developmental Delays." *Early Childhood Education Journal* 41 (4): 299–306.

"Storytellng, Story Acting, and Literacy in the Boston Public Schools: An Interview With Jason Sachs, Ben Mardell, & Marina Boni." 2014. *American Journal of Play* 6 (2): 173–89. www.journalofplay.org/sites/www.journalofplay.org/files/pdf-articles/6-2-interview-storytelling-story-acting-and-literacy_0.pdf.

Tannock, M.T. 2008. "Rough and Tumble Play: An Investigation of the Perceptions of Educators and Young Children." *Early Childhood Education Journal* 35 (4): 357–61.

Texas Association for the Education of Young Children. 2014. Special issue, *Early Years*, Spring.

Tucker, K. 2014. *Mathematics Through Play in the Early Years*. 3rd ed. Thousand Oaks, CA: SAGE.

Waite-Stupiansky, S., & M. Findlay. 2002. "The Fourth R: Recess and Its Link to Learning." *The Educational Forum* 66 (1): 16–25.

Weisberg, D.S., K. Hirsh-Pasek, & R.M. Golinkoff. 2013. "Guided Play: Where Curricular Goals Meet a Playful Pedagogy." *Mind, Brain, and Education* 7 (2): 104–12.

Widerstrom, A.H. 2005. *Achieving Learning Goals Through Play: Teaching Young Children With Special Needs*. International Issues in Early Intervention series. Baltimore, MD: Brookes.

Wilson, R. 2007. *Nature and Young Children: Encouraging Creative Play and Learning in Natural Environments*. 2nd ed. New York: Routledge.

Wohlwend, K.E. 2011. *Playing Their Way Into Literacies: Reading, Writing, and Belonging in the Early Childhood Classroom*. Language & Literacy series. New York: Teachers College Press.

Journal and Web Resources

American Journal of Play is a free peer-reviewed, online journal from The Strong National Museum of Play that examines play through a variety of perspectives, from early childhood to neuroscience to popular culture. Emerging research as well as historical perspectives are explored. The journal's archives, dating back to summer 2008, are available. www.journalofplay.org

KaBOOM! is a nonprofit dedicated to bringing active play into the daily lives of all children, especially those living in low-income communities. KaBOOM! creates great places to play, inspires communities, and works to drive the national discussion about the importance of play. kaboom.org

Let the Children Play promotes unstructured play and contains access to a monthly newsletter, links to early childhood blogs, and popular posts searchable by type of play. The "Play Outside!" section houses a database of photograph-oriented ideas for outdoor play. www.letthechildrenplay.net

NAEYC's Play and Children's Learning page highlights the latest research on play, articles that detail play's significance in children's learning and development and its role in the classroom, books about play, ideas about play to share with families, and other resources. www.naeyc.org/play

The Power of Play, from the Government of Newfoundland and Labrador's Department of Education and Early Childhood Development, offers links to a literature review, articles, posters, videos, and other resources about play. http://www.ed.gov.nl.ca/edu/earlychildhood/power.html

Reflections on Play: A Resource Guide is a webpage from the National Institute for Early Education Research's (NIEER) *Preschool Matters . . . Today!* blog. In March 2014, NIEER conducted a two-week blog forum on the importance of play in early childhood education. This site compiles forum posts from various experts in the field and offers a recommended reading list on play in early childhood. www.preschoolmatters.org/2014/03/07/reflections-on-play-a-resource-guide-2

The Strong National Museum of Play website offers museum information, indicating sources that include school lessons based on a topic, and links to play studies and reports. The physical museum, in Rochester, New York, offers a child-focused circulating library. www.museumofplay.org

Tips and Tools on Play is a webpage from Zero to Three containing links to information on play from birth to age 3. Parents and educators can find articles, brochures, podcasts, and slideshows. www.zerotothree.org/child-development/play/tips-and-tools-play.html

Reflecting, Discussing, and Exploring

Questions and Follow-Up Activities

Peter J. Pizzolongo

The articles in *Spotlight on Young Children: Exploring Play* provide guidance for early childhood educators who want to support and enhance children's learning through various kinds of play. Play is a teaching tool that supports learning and is an important vehicle for encouraging children to develop self-regulation. Play gives children opportunities to develop physical competence and to enjoy the outdoors. There is evidence that play helps children understand and make sense of their world, and understand and build academic concepts. The strategies in this book will help you support each child's learning through both child-guided and adult-guided play.

To help readers review and expand on the ideas in this book, we have developed this study guide—a series of questions and follow-up activities. First, we invite you to think about your own experiences learning through play. We then ask you to connect your early experiences to strategies for promoting children's learning through play. Specific questions and suggested activities related to each article follow. Finally, general questions about curriculum, teaching practices, resources, and next steps can help you pull together concepts and teaching strategies.

A. Recalling Your Own Early Experiences

1. Consider the kinds of play you engaged in as a child. Where and for how long did your play take place? Was it unstructured, sustained, facilitated, supervised? Were there times when you experienced what Csikszentmihalyi calls *flow* (see p. 88)? Record your play memories and reflections, including prose and sketches, in a journal. Discuss them with a friend or colleague, and note similarities and differences depending on age, culture, gender, and other factors.

Peter J. Pizzolongo is associate executive director for Professional Development Solutions at NAEYC. He is an author, trainer, and former teacher educator, program administrator, and teacher of young children.

2. What types of materials did you like to explore as a young child? How did the adults in your life promote your explorations? What could they have done differently to provide you with access to a greater range of materials? How might your experiences as a child affect the choice of materials you provide to the children in your setting?

3. Think about some of the benefits play offers for young children's development (social, emotional, cognitive, and physical) and ways that play supports their knowledge and skills in content areas. What kinds of play did you enjoy as a child that resulted in these benefits? As an adult, do you engage in play activities that have similar benefits?

B. Expanding on Each Article

Let's Get Messy! Learning Through Art and Sensory Play / Trudi Schwarz and Julia Luckenbill

Infants and toddlers benefit from hands-on exploration of art and sensory materials. The authors suggest strategies for planning a curriculum that includes these activities, encouraging experimentation while supervising exploration, and affirming the *process* of such activities for young children.

1. A child-centered approach to learning is important for planning art activities for infants and toddlers. What are three art or sensory activities you could plan for a group of infants under 12 months, infants 12–18 months, and toddlers ages 18–36 months? What might the children learn from these explorations?

2. What do you need to consider when planning these activities so that they respond to children's interests and are safe and age appropriate?

3. Sharing information with families about children's sensory and art explorations helps them understand what children learn through these activities. In your communications with families, what are some key points you can share about their children's activities and learning?

4. What are some ways you could extend or change activities in response to your observations of the children's initial explorations?

Lively Minds at Play: Planning Environments and Materials That Support the Way Young Children Learn / Deb Curtis, Kasondra L. Brown, Lorrie Baird, and Anne Marie Coughlin

Citing research that confirms toddlerhood as a time of immense development and learning, the authors observe and document toddlers' use of their "remarkable brains" as they explore items not usually provided for this age group. While acknowledging the necessity of supervising play closely, the authors offer principles for planning environments and choosing materials that encourage toddlers' expansive learning capacities.

5. How do you think the toddlers you work with experience the materials you provide for them? As you watch them interact with materials, what are they showing you that they know or know how to do?

6. Before reading the article, what was your typical response when children explored materials in ways different from their intended use? How do you think your reaction affected children's exploration and learning?

7. What current materials and experiences do you provide for toddlers? What seems to keep them engaged? After reading this article, what new materials and experiences do you want to offer to engage them for longer periods of time and in complex ways?

8. Review the section "Principles for Planning Environments and Choosing Materials" on page 23. With a colleague, brainstorm ways to implement these steps, and then put your plans into action. Document children's explorations through photographs and/or videos.

Assessing and Scaffolding Make-Believe Play / Deborah J. Leong and Elena Bodrova

Research provides much evidence of the positive effects that well-developed, adult-supported play has on various areas of children's development. The authors provide strategies for assessing the levels of preschool children's independent play to determine the appropriate level of teacher scaffolding.

9. According to Vygotsky and Elkonin, mature intentional make-believe play does not appear until children are in preschool and kindergarten. How is the play of infants and toddlers different from the play of preschoolers and kindergartners? What do children master in infancy and toddlerhood that are necessary steps in the development of higher-level make-believe play?

10. The article describes five stages in children's make-believe play development. Children may have some behaviors that fit in a higher or lower stage, but may be predominantly in one stage. Think of children you work with who are in one of these stages. What evidence do you see that the children are in this stage?

11. After assessing levels of children's play, teachers decide what kind of scaffolding is most appropriate for each child. List two ways you can scaffold children as they plan their play, take on and maintain roles, use props and language, and engage in scenarios.

12. Children use "role speech" when they are in stages 4 and 5. Vygotskians argue that in the use of this speech children actually talk like adults, using adult intonation and vocabulary. Think back to some of the role speech you have heard when children were acting out grownup roles. Did you observe examples of advanced grammar and vocabulary? How can you help children engage in and master role speech in their play?

"Where Do the Bears Go?" The Value of Child-Directed Play / Genan T. Anderson, Anita Rae Spainhower, and Ann C. Sharp

Child-directed play stories enable preschoolers to problem solve, make decisions, and self-regulate. The authors highlight ways in which children's play is enhanced with scaffolding and identify early learning standards that can be addressed in a play scenario.

13. What value does child-directed play have for developing literacy and math skills? How does such play provide opportunities for decision making?

14. If faced with the declaration from colleagues or staff members that "my children don't know how to play," how might you use this article to highlight specific teaching strategies to support and scaffold the emerging play skills of young children?

15. Child-directed play provides opportunities to build life skills such as problem solving and decision making. How and when during child-directed play does this occur?

Flying Over the School: Superhero Play—Friend or Foe? / Timothy A. Kinard

The author analyzes superhero play in preschool and addresses the philosophical, psychological, sociological, and anthropological foundations of such play. He looks at one school in which "teachers trust children to play with the powerful ideas involved in superhero play" and in the process help children make meaning from their experiences.

16. Rough-and-tumble superhero play can be disconcerting, alarming, or annoying to some teachers. How can you guide superhero play so that it supports children's self-regulatory skills, promotes high-level mature sociodramatic play, and enhances language development and use?

17. How do children respond when adults censor the themes that influence their play, their drawing, their writing, or their conversations? How can allowing superhero play encourage democratic participation in an early education setting?

18. If you, as a teacher, find that families or your principal, director, or colleagues are uncomfortable with the violence-tinged themes of the play in your setting, what new perspectives on play could you offer them? In crafting your answer, consider the perspectives the article offers in terms of executive function as well as the concept of teachers and children coconstructing knowledge by riffing off each other's ideas without censoring.

"Todos Vamos a Jugar, Even the Teachers"—Everyone Playing Together / Ysaaca Axelrod

This article describes the activities and interactions in a Head Start classroom where teachers support culturally and linguistically diverse children's dramatic play. The author highlights the intersection of play and language as well as ways teachers can integrate themselves into children's play while supporting and maintaining the integrity of the play.

19. In what ways does your program currently reflect the cultural and linguistic diversity of the children and the larger community? After reading this article, what new ideas do you have about making your program more inclusive of children's diversity? How do you think children and families will respond to these changes?

20. Reflect on ways you currently support children's play. After reading this article, what new strategies would you like to implement? For example, what are some ways you can observe and learn more about children while playing with them? How might this knowledge have a positive impact on your daily teaching practices?

21. Create a plan for introducing materials or interacting more frequently with children during play in ways that support their cultures and languages. For example, if children speak Spanish and enjoy playing doctor, learn vocabulary such as *médico* (doctor) and *Estoy enferma* (I'm sick) that you can use while assuming the role of patient.

Which Toys Promote High-Quality Play? Reflections on the Five-Year Anniversary of the TIMPANI Study / Jeffrey Trawick-Smith, Jennifer Wolff, Marley Koschel, and Jamie Vallarelli

The TIMPANI Study—Toys That Inspire Mindful Play and Nurture the Imagination—is a five-year investigation of play materials children use in preschool. The authors report on the results from the fifth year of the study, providing useful suggestions to teachers as they choose new play materials for their classrooms and support families' efforts to choose toys for their children.

22. What are some reasons children of diverse family backgrounds and of different genders sometimes use toys in different ways? What are the implications of this variance for teachers of young children?

23. What are some of the characteristics of toys that inspire higher-quality play? What are some examples of such toys that can be provided in early childhood settings?

24. What ideas can educators share with families for selecting toys? What ideas can families share with educators for equipping a classroom?

Art Play: Stories of Engaging Families, Inspiring Learning, and Exploring Emotions / M. Susan McWilliams, Ashley Brailsford Vaughns, Anne O'Hara, Loretta S. Novotny, and Theodora Jo Kyle

Inspired by a collage-caricature artist, the authors discuss art play, literacy development, family engagement programming, guided play, and the language of emotions. They explore strategies for intentionally guiding children's learning through art play in preschool through third grade and introducing vocabulary with activities related to children's books.

25. Hanoch Piven's book *Let's Make Faces* playfully guides children to find objects that are familiar to them and poses an open-ended challenge: making faces out of loose parts. Identify at least two children's books that similarly offer potential for facilitating art play. With a colleague or peer, share why the books inspire play, support creativity, or foster wonder while focusing on a concept.

26. Reflect on your current practice with children and share how you might implement new strategies to either promote playful learning of a specific objective or facilitate imaginative storytelling.

27. As shared in the article, art play was used with families as an engagement, community-building, and getting-to-know-you activity. How might the activity be modified or extended to meet a specific need of families in your program or to help build ties in the community?

Holding on to Play: Reflecting on Experiences as a Playful K–3 Teacher / Lisa D. Wood

The author shares her views on the importance of play and provides practical ways for educators to support children's play and communicate its value to others, including soliciting support for play-based learning, building a play language for advocacy, and making the benefits of play visible.

28. Think about the opportunities for play you currently provide during your daily program. Where do children play and for how long? How do you facilitate or supervise play? How are children responding?

29. What are some challenges you face when providing play opportunities? Why might these challenges exist? After reading this article, what new ideas do you have about ways to overcome these challenges so children have more opportunities for play?

30. How do you make the importance of play visible in your classroom? For example, in what ways do you communicate the value of play to families, colleagues, and community members? After reading this article, what new strategies do you want to try? How do you think people will respond?

31. The author discusses the importance of nurturing our own play as adults. What play activities do you engage in, and how might they affect your own development and your interactions with the children you work with?

Play for All Children: Access to Quality Play Experiences as a Social Justice Issue / Olga S. Jarrett, John Sutterby, Darlene DeMarie, and Vera Stenhouse

Access to play spaces in the United States is impacted by disparities related to race, class, and gender. This article summarizes several research studies on play and provides information to raise awareness regarding play experiences in kindergarten and primary classrooms.

32. As the authors describe, a visible area of injustice in the United States is access to quality play environments. Think of your experiences working in or observing programs for young children. How does the quality of children's play environments influence the types of play you have observed?

33. The NAEYC Code of Ethical Conduct notes that an early childhood educator's responsibilities include working "through education, research, and advocacy toward a society in which all young children have access to high-quality early care and education programs" (Ideal I-4.4). In addition, the Code states, "When we become aware of a practice or situation that endangers the health, safety, or well-being of children, we have an ethical responsibility to protect children or inform parents and/or others who can" (Principle P-4.7). How can you use the Code as a resource to address the issue of access to quality play experiences? (The Code can be found at www.naeyc.org/positionstatements/ethical_conduct.)

34. How can you communicate with families, community members, and other stakeholders in your area about the importance of access to quality play experiences? What measures will lead to the most change?

Big Body Play: Understanding and Supporting It / Frances M. Carlson

The author addresses misconceptions about rough play and ways in which it is distinctly different from fighting. She provides strategies for supporting rough play for children from infancy through third grade, including ensuring a safe, appropriate environment and developing policies and rules that support this play style.

35. How would you describe your understanding and acceptance of rough play? Did reading this article change your beliefs about it? If so, how? Given all the benefits this type of play offers children, how can you work toward becoming more accepting of it as a learning strategy for young children?

36. Examine both your indoor and outdoor play spaces in light of what you learned about children's rough play. What changes need to be made to more fully support this play style and ensure children's safety?

37. How will you communicate the value of children's rough play to families? For those concerned about their children engaging in such play, how can you assure them that this kind of play will be supervised and remain safe?

38. Review your state early learning standards (or other learning standards that guide your work with children). Which ones are addressed through children's rough play, especially when their play involves peers?

C. Making Connections

Consider the Big Picture

1. In your view, what are the three main themes or take-away messages in this collection of articles? Discuss your ideas with others to find commonalities and unique impressions.

2. Review the online supplemental article to this Spotlight book, "A Conversation About Play," by Peter Pizzolongo and Kyle Snow. (This article can be accessed at www.naeyc.org/books/spotlight_on_young_children_exploring_play_conversation.) The authors note that attempts to define or describe play invariably result in seemingly conflicting ideas: Play is something that children do "just because," and it is fun; or it is a way in which children learn. What are your thoughts on these two ways of looking at the role of play in children's lives?

3. Several of the articles provide examples of ways in which adults guide children's play. When is it most appropriate to do so? When might it be more appropriate to let children play without adult intervention or guidance?

4. How might you use the content of the articles to counter the claim that "in today's high-stakes early childhood programs, there is no longer time for play"?

Examine Curriculum Goals and Expected Outcomes

5. Read NAEYC's position statement titled "Developmentally Appropriate Practice in Early Childhood Programs Serving Children From Birth Through Age 8" (2009), which focuses on appropriate strategies for guiding children's learning, including play (see www.naeyc.org/files/naeyc/file/positions/PSDAP.pdf). In particular, review the principles of child development and learning (principle 10 on p. 14 addresses play); and guideline 2 on teaching, on pages 17–20. How does the position statement support what you have learned from the articles in this collection? How do your program practices align with NAEYC's position statement on developmentally appropriate practice, and specifically guideline 2? What could you do differently to better support the guideline?

6. How does the content of the articles relate to your curriculum, assessment system and tools, learning standards your program follows (e.g., the Common Core State Standards, your state's early learning standards, the Head Start Child Development and Early Learning Framework), or other requirements applicable to your setting?

Use Reflection to Enhance Teaching Practices

7. Which ideas presented in the articles or raised in your discussions affirm your work with or on behalf of young children and families? Which ideas cause you to think about ways to build on your current practices to promote learning through play? Which ideas cause you to question your practices and consider alternatives that would better promote learning through play?

8. What does research indicate about what children learn through play? What does research say about the relationship between play and children's learning across the domains: cognitive, language and literacy, social, emotional, and physical development?

9. Several articles included vignettes that offer an adult's observations of children's play. How do you use observation to assess what children are learning as they engage in child-guided play? How do you document your observations and, with other forms of evidence, use them to prepare the environment and plan your interactions with children to build on their learning through play?

10. In what ways do children bring their cultural experiences into their play? How can play support children's understanding of cultures different from their own? How can you support children's cultural experiences in your setting?

11. Why is it important for teachers to be active participants in children's play?

Focus on Families and Communities

12. The articles provide guidance for adults who work with or on behalf of young children regarding the role of play as a learning strategy. How can you use this information to prepare for conversations with families, program administrators, and others regarding the importance of play in children's lives?

13. Partnering with families to promote consistency between what happens in a child's home and the early childhood setting is important. How can you support families in promoting their children's learning through play outside of the program?

14. Connect families to online resources for supporting children's play. A few suggestions are NAEYC's For Families site (http://families.naeyc.org/), the "Play and Learning" topics page on the NAEYC site (www.naeyc.org/play), the PBS Parents site (www.pbs.org/parents/child-development), and Zero to Three (www.zerotothree.org).

Identify Resources and Plan Next Steps

15. Review the resource list provided in this book (starting on p. 119). Make a note of what you have read and found useful. Share these with your colleagues. Create a new list for yourself of additional resources that others recommend to you.

16. With others, choose one article or book and one online resource that none of you has used. Make plans to read or review these resources and meet later to discuss your reactions on ways to implement what you have learned.

17. Over a period of a few weeks, observe, document, and take photographs or videos of children engaged in play. Add the observations and images to your reflective journal. Review your journal and look for patterns. What play properties do the children display? What types of play personalities do you notice? (Play properties and play personalities are discussed in Lisa Wood's article, "Holding on to Play: Reflecting on Experiences as a Playful K–3 Teacher," on p. 87.) Determine to what extent the curriculum and environment are supporting children's play and what additional strategies you could use to extend their play and learning experiences.

18. Refer again to the online supplemental article to this Spotlight book, "A Conversation About Play," by Peter Pizzolongo and Kyle Snow (see p. 127 for the URL). The authors reference the concept of children learning in multiple ways: Valued content is learned through investigation, play, and focused, intentional teaching. Children learn by exploring, thinking about, and inquiring about all sorts of phenomena. These experiences help children investigate 'big ideas, those that are important at any age and are connected to later learning. Early education is not *either* play *or* learning: It is *both/and*, which is a fundamental concept of developmentally appropriate practice. Discuss with your colleagues the types of activities—and for which children—you see as most appropriate as teacher guided and those most appropriate as child guided (which children primarily engage in as play). Incorporate these ideas into your curriculum planning over the coming weeks and months.

19. Many questions regarding the ways in which children best learn different concepts and skills are yet to be answered—by researchers, educators, and other stakeholders in the field. What questions do you still have after reading these articles and completing the suggested tasks in this study guide? Create a plan of action for your own professional development, including what resources you need, where you can find them, with whom can you discuss your questions, and what you want to accomplish in your teaching practice.